Becoming an Orchard

Fruit Bearing Strategies for Any Church

By

Bryan D. Collier

PRESS

Becoming an Orchard
by Bryan D. Collier

Printed in the United States of America

ISBN 1-60034-001-6

www.xulonpress.com

Table of Contents

Acknowledgements

*N*o work would be possible without the extreme patience and overwhelming support of my family. Wendy, thanks for always saying, "Yes" with me to God's call. Olivia and Houston, thanks for reminding me of the stuff dreams are made of. I love all three of you more than words can say.

A special thank you to my friend Roger Weldon, who after writing his own book, would not let me rest until I had written mine; thanks for reminding me continually that I am not sick, and that I do not have a problem—even when sometimes I am pretty sure I do!

Finally to The Orchard family, its staff, leaders and people, thank you for believing in this dream enough that you were willing to try it. It is my life's privilege to be your pastor and friend. God teaches me daily through you.

CHAPTER 1

My Dream Church

Twenty-five pages entitled "My Dream Church;" that was the first assignment of my first doctor of ministry class in the summer of 1997. I was perfectly clear about the topic. However, I was equally unclear about what I would write. Church was what church was, there wasn't very much room for dreaming and so I had no idea what my dream church looked like. If someone were to give you a blank sheet of paper and instruct you to write about your dream church, what would you write? If someone were to give you complete freedom to create any kind of church you wanted, what would you create? Most of us would be as confused as I was that first day of class.

Earlier, in the spring of 1997, I received word that I had been selected as a Beeson Pastor Fellow in Asbury Theological Seminary's Doctor of Ministry Program. This one of a kind program paid for me to take a year long sabbatical for study and growth in the areas of Biblical Preaching and Christian Leadership. This year of study was to be to be followed by a two-year dissertation writing process as I returned to full-time ministry.

I enthusiastically made the move to seminary enthralled by the idea of study, travel and interaction with some of the world's finest church leaders. The one thing I was most unsure about, however, was what the focus of my writing and study would be. However, all that became clear to me thirteen pages into Peter Senge's book, *The Fifth Discipline*.

I don't remember why I began reading the book when I did, but I remember clearly the joy and pain that I felt as Senge described the feeling that people get when being part of a great team. He writes:

> When you ask people what it is like being part of a great team, what is most striking is the meaningfulness of the experience. People talk about being part of something larger than themselves, of being connected, of being generative. It becomes quite clear that, for many, their experiences as part of truly great teams stand out as singular periods of life lived to the fullest. Some spend the rest of their lives looking for ways to recapture that spirit. The most accurate word in Western culture to describe what happens in a learning organization...is metanoia and it means shift of mind. The word has a rich history. For the Greeks it meant a fundamental shift or change, or more literally transcendence of mind. In early Christian tradition it took on a special meaning of awakening a shared intuition and direct knowing of the highest of God. (13)

With the reading and hearing of those words, joy was felt, disappointment was stirred and a dream was born. I was overjoyed for such a well-respected business mind to recognize that the early Christian tradition probably had a better understanding of learning organizations than anyone. However, my disappointment began to rise when I realized that for the most part those words could not be said about the current Christian communities of faith. My disappointment only deepened as I read the next 350 pages and found not one additional mention of the Church as an example—I felt this was, primarily, because none warranted mentioning. In those moments, God began to stir within me a dream that would become The Orchard.

It was my passionate desire that a community of faith could reclaim its birthright as a congregation that existed in a state of metanoia. Meaning this community of faith would be so in tune with God's call and passion that it would be pliable enough to reshape itself continually in order to remain a useful instrument to accomplish God's purposes. It would have a God centered intuitiveness about how to communicate the eternal truth of the Good News to an ever changing culture. This community of faith would not be encumbered by the politics of power, and personal opinion would not be the deciding factor in matters of governance. This community of faith would clearly speak the message of faith in the language of the people, and it would hold everything—every tradition, every practice, every movement—lightly while holding to the unchanging Gospel message firmly. This community of faith would exist for outsiders, and the dress, the music, the décor, the mindset of its leaders would be adjusted accordingly. This would be a community of faith who had a clear understanding of what God was calling them to do, and how God was calling them uniquely to do it. Moreover, this would be a people whose structure was streamlined enough to actually be this kind of community and not merely talk or dream about it.

The Orchard is that community of faith. For seven years now, I have had the privilege of leading a vibrant church that is reaching the Tupelo Region for Christ in an amazing way.

In June of 1998, my wife, Wendy, and I were sent to Tupelo to begin a new United Methodist Church. A few weeks after moving to town, we met with an assembled group of twenty-four people interested in being a part of that work. Over the next few weeks, a number of them decided they did not want to be a part of the church as we articulated it. The good news, however, was that the ones who remained brought their friends. That core group grew to almost ninety people in the next five months and we launched on December 6th with 256 people in worship.

Over the next few weeks, our attendance dropped gradually to 140, but beginning with week five, The Orchard began steadily growing, and has continued to grow for seven years. Today, we currently average over 2,000 weekly in worship and almost 2,500 people call The Orchard their home. There have been hundreds of people who have made first time commitments to Jesus and engaged in growing as his disciple. Hundreds of children have been baptized as parents have acknowledge God's claiming of their child, and hundreds more have begun to make regular worship attendance and small group involvement a priority in their lives.

Numbers cannot begin to describe the life change that is happening in the Tupelo area because God is blessing and using The Orchard. A few of the stories of these changed lives appear in the pages that follow, they are representative of the hundreds, and hundreds of others whose stories could appear were there space. If you were to attend one of our worship services and begin to ask individuals their Orchard story, you would find that almost everyone has a story of change to tell.

This became clear to me during a search process for one of our senior staff openings. The Leadership Team was conducting the final interview with the candidate, and they asked him why he wanted to be part of what was going on at The Orchard. He took several minutes to reply, but closed his remarks by turning the question on them. What was it about The Orchard that made them want to be a part? The fifteen member leadership team spoke for the next hour, and had we not stopped, it would have gone on for another hour!

It is not uncommon for a wife to stop by the office just to say, "Thank you for starting The Orchard. My husband didn't go to church for the first 15 years of our marriage, but now he is the first one out of the bed on Sunday mornings." I am routinely stopped in Wal-Mart by someone who attends The Orchard just so they can tell me how much they are being blessed by The Orchard or how much God has changed their life because of their attendance.

Last year I was officiating at a wedding, and I sat next to one of the groomsmen at the rehearsal dinner. A few minutes into our conversation he suddenly realized that I was the pastor at The Orchard (the wedding was offsite), and so he pointedly asked me if that was where I pastored. I said that I did, and after answering, I had one of the most profound moments in all my pastoral life. He said, "Thank you for helping me." He continued, "Last year I needed to go to drug rehab. I could not afford it, but The Orchard helped pay for me to go and now I have my life back." I sat there speechless. After some moments of quiet, I fumbled out, "I am glad we could help," and in my heart I said a prayer of thanksgiving for the opportunity to pastor a church like that.

The last seven years have been a dream for me. I wrote the "My Dream Church" paper, but more importantly, by God's grace I began to live out that dream so that now twenty-five pages do not begin to tell the story.

Words cannot capture and numbers cannot quantify the tremendous ways that God is using The Orchard. The pages that follow include some of the stories and many of the lessons that God has shown us along the way. My desire is that God will use these stories and principles to inspire you and your community of faith to dream about and to act in ways that mean greater effectiveness for the Kingdom of Christ. Maybe you will be able to apply one or two of the ideas that I share, or maybe God will lead you to discover many new ideas from the time spent with this book. Either way my prayer is that God will continue to work in our lives and our communities of faith, and that we will be responsive to that work in order that all may come to know Him so that every church may *Become an Orchard* overflowing with Kingdom fruit.

Chapter 2

A Face not a Place

*O*ne of the most significant decisions in the history of The Orchard was made before we launched our first worship service. My wife, Wendy, and I were sent to Tupelo, Mississippi in June of 1998 to start a new United Methodist Congregation. Within the first week, we met with a small group of people interested in helping launch this new community of faith and soon began to divide those people into task groups with responsibilities for differing segments of the launch. There were nine groups, and each group had a leader to whom I primarily related; I personally led the marketing group. I maintained a close connection to this aspect of the launch because those first people had never seen a congregation with the characteristics we were envisioning. Furthermore, none of them, outside of a church listing its service times in the religion section of the local newspaper or yellow pages, had ever seen a church use marketing to attract constituents.

Initially, we turned to a marketing company that produced professional grade commercials with a general message and an edited tag at the end of the commercial relaying the church's service times, location or message. We previewed numerous sample commercials and chose one that was funny and that poked fun at cultural understandings of what went on in church. Then we spent a few hours deciding what information we wanted to use in our tag. Weeks later, we received our commercial and gathered to watch it. Our responses, however, were much different than any of us could have anticipated—it was too "slick." The company promised to deliver an excellent, quality product, and they certainly made good on their promise. However, each of us knew, internally, that it would not connect to the people in our community. Although technically excellent in every way, the people in the commercial were not like anyone we knew. It was a stark and eye-opening reality.

Given the hours it took to develop the original ad, it was all the more shocking that, in less than an hour, we developed a new marketing idea and at the same time a marketing philosophy. We decided to point people toward our convictions not just a place. We decided to put faces in our advertising. Instead of letting someone else do the talking for us, we decided that we would speak for ourselves. We would not have to find something someone said in a canned commercial, but could carefully craft a message that communicated to our target group exactly who we were and how they could connect to us. We decided that we would never do our preaching in our marketing but that our "preaching" would take place in our lives and through our relationships. Our marketing, then was for attracting people to a relationship where our preaching could happen. From that day on, we never tried to connect people to a place (especially since our place was always moving in the early days); our desire was to connect them to a face.

This guiding principle has been one of the most significant decisions at The Orchard. It not only affects our marketing, it affects our entire ministry. In marketing and in ministry we focus on relationships.

Priority of Need

I do not need to tell you that one of humanity's greatest needs is for relationship. This need exemplifies what it means to be created in the image of God. God said let us make people in our image, to be like ourselves. Notice the choice of words: "God said; let *us* make *people...*" God's description of his intent was stated in the plural. The original is, "let us make *man*," which is the Hebrew word for human beings. In any case, God's intention was not just one, but at least more than one. Why? God exists in relationship—Father, Son and Holy Spirit, and if we are going to be in the image of God, we have to exist in relationship. Some may instantly think of the marriage relationship, but our need for relationship exceeds even that most holy of covenants. What this "made for relationship" nature means is that we cannot exist alone as a person of faith. This truth is seen repeatedly in Scripture:

- Solomon points out this need for Spiritual connectedness: "As iron sharpens Iron, a friend sharpens a friend." (Proverbs 27.17)
- In Ecclesiastes, Solomon again writes: Two people can accomplish more than twice as much as one; they get a better return for their labor. If one person falls, the other can reach out and help. But people who are alone when they fall are in real trouble. And on a cold night, two under the same blanket can gain warmth from each other. But how can one be warm alone? A person standing alone can be attacked and defeated, but two can stand back-to-back and conquer. Three are even better, for a triple-braided cord is not easily broken. "Two are better than one, because they have a good return for their work: If one falls down, his friend can help him up. But pity the man who falls and has no one to help him up! Also, if two lie down together, they will keep warm. But how can one keep

17

warm alone? Though one may be overpowered, two can defend themselves. A cord of three strands is not quickly broken." (4.9-12)

- When the time came for a strategic decision during His ministry, Jesus made an interesting choice. He gathered 70 workers, like regional representatives, and sent them to various towns to prepare people for His visits (see Luke 10:1). He could have sent each disciple separately and reached more towns. Instead, He chose to send those disciples in teams of two. An efficiency expert might criticize that decision for duplicating effort and cutting productivity in half, but Jesus knew that some ministries are performed best by two, not one. When two people work together, one can protect the other. One can encourage another. Two can split the work, offset each other's weaknesses, and draw on each other's strengths. Companionship makes two more effective, not less, than one.

Even the completeness enjoyed by the Father, Son and Holy Spirit as individuals is gracefully submitted to the whole because of God's design for relationship. The Father works by his Son and by his Spirit, who, in turn, point to each other as a means for validating and celebrating the relationship. Imagine the possibilities if we could live like that!

True, sometimes it is not easy to be in relationships, because none of our relationships reflect the completeness of the Father, Son, and Holy Spirit (The Trinity), and oftentimes, the cost of relationship is very great. However, the reward is far more significant than the price because of our design for relationship.

General William Westmoreland was reviewing a platoon of paratroopers in Vietnam, and as he went down the line, he asked each of them the question: "How do you like jumping, son?" "Love it, sir!" was the first answer. "How do you like jumping?" he asked the next. "The greatest experience in my life, sir!" exclaimed the paratrooper. "How do you like jumping?" he asked the third. "I hate it, sir," he replied. "Then why do you do it?" asked Westmoreland. "Because I want to be around guys who love to jump." (Harvey MacKay, *Swim with the Sharks*). We are made for relationship!

Sadly, this design for relationship can also lead us down a destructive path. Often the cost of relationships takes a toll on our lives, because we have tried to substitute earthly relationships for the primary relationship God created us for—relationship with Him! Saint Augustine said, "There is a God shaped void in each of us that cannot be satisfied by another…only by God."

Our desire for and reliance upon relationship is evidence that we are created by God, in His image and that longing can only be satisfied by directing it first to God. Then and only then, can we begin to enter into right relationships with those around us.

It is our desire for relationship that confirms we are made in the image of God. However, the inverse is also true. Our broken relationships testify that the primary focus in our relationships is out of balance. The Body of Christ is where a person finds that right balance. But to be able to talk to people about what needs to be their primary relationship, you have to first establish a relationship with them.

Our society has never been more fractured, more indi-vidualistic, or more self-serving, likewise, never has our society been in more denial about its loneliness. We were created for, seek out naturally, and have a deep longing to be in relationship.

Who will mediate this human-divine relationship if not the community of faith? The Church must fully comprehend this need and prioritize accordingly for connecting people to faces and not places.

Connecting at The Orchard

At The Orchard, we have made some unique moves to enhance this opportunity to connect people in relationships. In the first year of The Orchard, we held "Coffee Houses." We would bring lots of food and coffee, and open up the microphone for improv talent. Some nights, we might have a band or even karaoke, in order to provide an atmosphere where people could get to know one another better. These gatherings were great fun, but were even more amazing in their power to transform strangers into friends.

During the first six years of our existence, we took a ten-minute break after the first twenty minutes of our service. We would kick off our service with music and prayers for the whole family. Then, after the morning pastoral prayer we would take a break and let people exit the worship space to settle their children in children's church (GrowZone or Sprout Patch) and grab a cup of coffee and maybe even say, "hello," to one or two people before we once again started the service. We also serve donut holes every Sunday—we all know that it is easier to talk to someone with a mouthful of food! This unique part of our Sundays was highlighted by the Local Baptist Association and encouraged among their churches! This break became such an important part of our relationship building that in 2004 we moved it between our two services and lengthened it so that people could have more time to relate.

Our ministries are also relationship oriented. Because of this priority on relationships, The Orchard is a church of small groups. In our small groups, we hope that five things happen: Discipleship, Outreach, Community, Shepherding and Leadership Development. All of these things happen in relationship as one person encourages the development of another. None of these things happen at a particular place... they all happen because of a face to face connection.

It has been easy to visually communicate this "face not a place" concept at The Orchard because we began without a building. When you are meeting in rented facilities and constantly moving from facility to facility (some very much less than ideal) during the startup phase, it is much easier to say, "The church is not a place." For the first three years, The Orchard met in an 80,000 square foot furniture hall. We had plenty of space, but it was all one room. On many Sundays, our nursery was a hallway with a table turned down at each end to keep the kids from escaping. It is easy, and oftentimes imperative, to look beyond the surroundings and find the church in hearts, not mortar.

During the next four years, The Orchard met in a rented warehouse, again one large room, to which we added children's rooms and nurseries. It served us very well, but it too was less than ideal. However, it continually taught us the value of church being "faces not places." The Orchard recently moved into its first permanent facility. Like any church, the challenge to maintain the focus on people will be difficult; however, it is worth the effort. We understand clearly the incredible priority for relationship; it is the characteristic that has made our congregation thrive, and we dare not forget it.

A Much Needed Reputation

The result of an intentional focus on relationships will serve your congregation well. Your investment in relationships will provide your congregation with the reputation for being an open, caring place where people are welcome and lives are changed. The pastor should always propagate this idea. Work it into sermons, make it part of your announcements, wrap up your service with it. Instill in people both the desire and confidence to invite people to church who are far from God and need His grace. A church's commitment to relationships ignites the laity's passion for reaching out and gives them the assurance that whomever they invite will be welcome.

In Addition

A relational atmosphere also helps your preaching. By the time I stand up to preach, people have been welcomed, fed, encouraged, smiled at and relaxed. Now how do you think they receive the message? Remember I said earlier, "We don't do our preaching in our advertising. We do our attracting with our advertising?" Now do you understand why? Because we would never communicate such an important personal message through an impersonal means like advertising. The art of relationship building is too important.

Relating also helps your leading. When you give full attention and focus to relationships, the relational temperature and trust level of your church increases dramatically. And when the trust level is deservedly high, the church thrives because it spends no time second-guessing the leadership.

Each year we prepare the upcoming year's budget in November. And each year after that budget is approved we make it available to the entire congregation. The information in our budget, including salaries, is public information, and anyone connected to our church is welcome to it. The first couple of years, after our budget was completed, we printed approximately fifty copies and placed them at our information center for distribution. No one picked them up. We announced the availability again the second week—again, nobody picked them up. The congregation trusts the leaders of our congregation. They believe we are in such a relationship mindset, that they trust how we spend and allocate the resources entrusted to our care. Today, we still offer people a copy of the budget; however, rarely does anyone make such a request.

One other important aspect of how this focus on faces, not places affects your leading—it helps you squelch rumors or gossip. When I stand before our leaders or our congregation and say, "this did or did not happen." They believe me. Now, I have to work hard at making sure I am honoring their trust.

Even then, because of our relationship, they know that if I discover that I was wrong, I will come back and tell them so.

Conclusion

It takes capital to get any new venture off the ground. That is true of churches just like it is a business. However, the wise church, the church that will grow beyond imagination is the one that focuses on relational capital. These churches communicate that faces, not places are the critical dynamic in church life.

CHAPTER 3

Don't Find a Niche; Create One!

❖══❖

*A*pple Computers is one of the most creative organizations on planet earth. Many of their print and media advertisements were very simple and to the point. A few years ago, they came out with an aggressive advertising campaign that issued one of the most amazing challenges. The ads I am speaking of carried a picture of their distinctive Apple logo and the text consisted of two words: "Think Different." While I celebrate the incredible creativity and challenge of such an ad campaign, when it comes right down to it, thinking differently is not enough. We have to not only "Think Different." We have to "Be Different." This is especially true for the church.

It is easy enough to argue that Jesus instructs the community of faith to be countercultural. However, often we have simply created a parallel culture of our own that is as lifeless and misdirected as the culture we stand against! One of the reasons our churches are empty is their predictability. People know what to expect from church. Same songs, same rituals, same time, same place, same sermon that leaves them confused, same...*well* you get the idea! One of the things that has helped The Orchard break out is a *raging* against the humdrum.

When then Bishop of The Mississippi Area of The United Methodist Church, Reverend Jack Meadors asked if I wanted to go to Tupelo to start a new church, my first response was an unequivocal "yes!" However, my follow up response was that I did not want to go to Tupelo to simply start another United Methodist Church. Tupelo already had six United Methodist Churches. Their worship styles covered the known worship spectrum. From the country church on the edge of the city to the high church downtown, there was something for everyone. I dreamed of was something that was outside of the known spectrum for Tupelo.

Dreaming and finding a niche are imperative in churches that are seeking to make a kingdom difference. When I moved to Tupelo there were statistically twenty-thousand (20,000) people who did not go to church. At first, other United Methodist Churches offered to help us by populating our new church by sending us numerous families. While I appreciated their offer, I quickly told them that we simply wanted two missional families from each congregation who shared our heart for reaching the 20,000 people in our area who did not have a personal relationship with Jesus or a connection to a community of faith. This "niche" fully encompassed half the population of our city and it would take an intentional effort by the other half to reach them!

Now you can see why niche making is imperative. If every niche were filled in any given town, then a large percentage of people would worship regularly at a church of their choice. The large percentage that do not are a testimony that they are not interested in the good news *as it is communicated in their town*. True, some won't be interested no matter how it is communicated! However, there are many who are hungry for the good news of the gospel, but they are either incapable of understanding it, or disinterested in it as they understand it! This truth should give us hope for reaching those people and an even greater desire to find out how to communicate the timeless truths of the good news in a time-conscious vernacular.

Thinking Different

Though I believe Apple did not go far enough, they did have it half right. Being different begins with thinking different—which I am confident was their unstated, desired response!

Paul's letter to the Romans includes these words: "Dear brothers and sisters, I plead with you to give your bodies to God. Let them be a living and holy sacrifice—the kind he will accept. When you think of what he has done for you, is this too much to ask? Don't copy the behavior and customs of this world, but let God transform you into a new person by changing the way you think..." (12:1-2). Clearly, Paul instructs that the key to living a certain way—as a living sacrifice—and the key to not conforming to the world begins with letting God change the way we think! Paul knew that if we were to ever be different, we would have to think different.

I don't want to stretch Paul's instruction too far, but can we agree that this is true with an organization as well as an individual? Mensa is an organization whose members have an IQ of 140 or higher. A few years ago, while at a convention in San Francisco, several members lunched at a local café. During the meal they discovered that their salt-shaker contained pepper and their peppershaker was full of salt. The group debated how they could swap the contents of the bottles without spilling, but use only the implements at hand? Clearly this was a job for Mensa! Each member presented ideas. Finally, they developed a brilliant solution involving a napkin, a straw, and an empty saucer. They called the waitress over to dazzle her with their solution. "Ma'am," they said, "We couldn't help but notice that the peppershaker contains salt and the saltshaker—""Oh," the waitress interrupted, much to the dismay of the resident geniuses. "Sorry about that." She then unscrewed the caps of both bottles and switched them. The church must begin to think differently about its communication and image problem. There is far too much at stake to do otherwise.

One final word on this need for a niche: When my three-year-old son, Houston, was in potty training, he asked, "Daddy, why don't people just go in their pants? My quick response was, "Because we just don't do that." But, after thinking about it, I begin to wonder myself. After some reflection, it occurred to me that the reason we don't go to the bathroom in our pants is that at sometime someone brought it to our attention that it would make more sense and be far more sanitary to go in this porcelain fixture mounted to the floor. Go figure—a cosmic question answered with practical thinking.

The people far from God in our communities are evidence that something different needs to happen. Our choice as the community of faith is either to make changes or keep "stinking things up."

Being Different

Charles Haddon Spurgeon once observed: The upper galleries at Versailles are filled with portraits, many of them extremely valuable and ancient. These are the likenesses of the greatest people of all lands and ages, drawn by the ablest artists. Yet more visitors wander through the rooms with little or no interest. In fact, after noticing one or two of the more prominent pictures, they hasten through the suite of chambers and descend to the other floors. Notice the change when the sightseers come to fine paintings like those of Horace Vernet, where the men and women are not inactive portraits but are actively engaged. There, the warrior who was passed by without notice upstairs is seen hewing his way to glory over heaps of slain, or the statesman is observed delivering weighty words before an assembly of princes and peers. Not the people but their actions engross attention. Portraits have no charm when scenes of stirring interest are set in rivalry with them. After all, then, let us be who or what we may, we must push ourselves or be mere nobodies, chips in the porridge, forgotten shells on the beach. If we would impress we must act. The dignity of standing still will never win the prize; we must run for it. Our influence over our times will arise mainly from our doing and suffering the will of God, not from our office or person. Life, life in earnest, life for God—this will tell on the age. But mere orderliness and propriety, inactive and passionless, will be utterly inoperative.

What makes The Orchard so distinctive is that its leaders and people have not been content to merely think differently, but they have genuinely pushed beyond the limits of thinking to being and ultimately beyond being to doing.

How do you discover your niche?

It might be easiest to say first a word about how you do not discover or create your own niche. The surest way to fail in this endeavor is imitation. Now it is widely stated that imitation is the sincerest form of flattery. It is also the sincerest way not to find your unique thumbprint. It appears obvious—imitation necessarily excludes uniqueness. But you would be surprised (or maybe not) how many churches, in an effort to creatively distinguish their ministries, actually end up copying others. That is not to say that other's ministries shouldn't inspire us or that we shouldn't gain insight into our circumstance by looking at other creative examples, but imitation excludes uniqueness and, as importantly, does not take into account the contextual differences.

Let me suggest a different process—one I have delineated as insight, interpretation and application. Insight asks, "What can I learn from this ministry? What ideas does this inspire?" Close on the heels, interpretation inquires, "What parts would work in my context? What parts wouldn't?" Finally, application directs "What does this ministry look like in my context?"

At The Orchard, although hundreds of congregations have influenced our thinking, I can point to the influences of five congregations in particular. The five are: The United Methodist Church of The Resurrection (COR) in Leawood, Kansas, Ginghamsburg United Methodist Church in Tipp City, Ohio; Mosaic in East Los Angeles, California; Saddleback Valley Community Church in Orange County, California and Willow Creek Community Church in South Barrington, Illinois. We learned something substantial from each of these congregations but carbon-copied nothing. For example, in our area, churches don't market to the surrounding community. One of the things we learned from The United Methodist Church of The Resurrection was that an excellent marketing strategy works wonders for putting your church on the minds of people who may attend church at sometime in the future. That truth was our insight. Our interpretation questions led us to believe that, like COR, mailouts of over-sized posters might work well in our area, but the phones-for-you program they used would not work well at all. Our application was to work out an extended and detailed mass mailer plan for putting our congregation on the minds of our community — just in case they decided to attend a church in the future!

Musically

One of the most important places for your congregation to be unique is musically. Next to the sermon (and maybe including the sermon) the reason people return (or don't return) to your church is their connection to the music. The Orchard has a distinct musical style. We sing a lot of music from the Passion Movement, but our music has more of a Nashville than an L.A. edge to it. The important thing about our congregation's musical style is that it is unique to our community. There are plenty of churches that sing hymns. Even one or two that chant the Psalms and some even have styles that would be described as inspirational or Gospel. But when we began our congregation one of the things that set us apart was that you could not hear our kind of music anywhere else in town, except maybe at the local bar or nightclub..

Whatever you do, don't underestimate the power of music to communicate truth to seekers. Which do you think they will remember throughout the week—your perfectly turned phrase in the sermon or the song about God being the only one they need?

Dress

In contrast to the "casual summer" dress that is becoming popular at most churches, The Orchard has always encouraged people to come wearing whatever they have to wear. On any given Sunday at The Orchard, we have people in slacks and golf shirts and people in tie-dye and beach sandals. The Deep South Bible belt seems to be the last place to adopt religious change, but even in the Deep South, dress expectations are shifting. Take the leap—remove the excuse of "I don't have anything to wear to church" from the list of reasons people believe they can't attend.

It is also important for the pastor to set the standard. People will not feel the freedom to come as they are, if you don't come as you are. My advice is this—punt the robe, punt the tie, punt the coat (unless it is cold!). I wear jeans or khaki's almost every Sunday. Think about what your target person might have to wear and wear the same. A little incarnational dressing might go a long way to getting them to experience the real thing!

Organizationally

One of the things I believe that discourages people from creatively thinking about ministry is the myriads of approvals needed to turn an idea into action. It is not uncommon in our denomination (UMC) for there to be at least five levels of approval required before people are let loose with their ministry idea. Most people can't or won't, endure that much suffering!

The way your church is organized structurally, profoundly affects the church's ability to act differently. So, set up your boards and approval systems to streamline ministry. Don't give tacit approvals, but make approval thorough, directive and quick! Create systems that allow for moving quickly from idea to action.

At The Orchard, ideas or initiatives presented to ministry leaders must satisfy three questions: (1) Does it have the potential to produce fruit for Christ's Kingdom?; (2) Does it help someone grow deep in the love of Jesus or branch out to others with that love?; (3) Is it in line with our core values? If the answer is yes, the proposed initiative goes straight to our Leadership Team for approval. When people are freely allowed to bring their ideas to the table, a congregation's ability to produce unique, successful ministries increases exponentially.

Logos and Taglines

One of the most significant ways you can communicate your uniqueness is by developing a distinct congregational identity. At The Orchard, our tree and roots logo is known all over town. One of my favorite stories was told to me by a dad, who was helping his six-year-old daughter put on her Timberland hikers one day and she said, "Look dad, my Orchard shoes!" The Timberline and our logo are similar enough that the connection was evident. If you ask me, a sure sign that we were moving in the right direction.

Few churches do this at all, and those who do, rarely do it well. United Methodist Churches all seem content to use the denominational cross and flame symbol. Please don't misunderstand; it is a fantastic symbol. Its imagery is distinctive, and when you see it, you know that you are seeing a United Methodist Church. However, in a town where six different United Methodist Churches are using it, the distinctive variable of a particular congregation is greatly reduced. Some will argue that this is good for the denomination. But, keep in mind, if the goal is to reach a particular target audience, and the style of your church is deliberately distinct from others of like denomination, the uniqueness of your logo matters. Denominational symbols are useful in identifying the similarities of a congregation, but share little with the observer as to why they should chose a particular congregation to call home.

The Orchard's tree with deep roots communicates who we are —Growing Deep and Branching Out. Which leads us to our next communication emphasis—a distinctively communicated mission statement. Consider these:

- The Orchard: Growing Deep. Branching Out
- Asbury Church: Living Out the Great Commission by Living Loud for the Greatest Commandment.
- Willow Creek Community Church, South Barrington, Illinois: To turn irreligious people into fully devoted followers of Jesus Christ.
- Mosaic, East Los Angeles: A Community of Faith, Love, and Hope
- The United Methodist Church of the Resurrection, Leawood, Kansas: To build a Christian community where non-religious and nominally religious people are becoming deeply committed Christians.

What is the distinctive focus of your congregation...do you know? Can you state it? If not, it is highly unlikely anyone else can either. These statements communicate the unique identity of your congregation.

Imagine someone getting into a conversation with an Orchard attendee. In the conversation, The Orchard attendee mentions their church. Their friend says inquisitively, "Tell me about your church." Now in addition to all that the person who attends The Orchard might say about the inspiring music, the great kid's ministries, the exciting youth ministries, the donuts, or the coffee, they will also say, "It is a place that helps people grow deep in the love of Jesus, and branch out to others with that love." That phrase is the hook. Because people may be drawn into the conversation about music ministries and food—but the extra is this...we want to help people "grow deep and branch out" and such a clear purpose is not what they expected from a church at all.

Ruining Church

On our fifth birthday in December of 2003, I stood before The Orchard and cast a vision for our congregation that we would be in the business of ruining church. It was an image I had mentioned from time to time, but, on this occasion, I wanted to be very intentional about it. My objective: Let our goal this next year be to *"Ruin Church" for everybody.* I challenged the congregation to ruin people's perceptions. People think "church" and assign all kinds of labels: irrelevant, meaningless, unhelpful, mean-spirited, comatose, stiff, just want something from me. I want to ruin those perceptions.

I also challenged The Orchard to ruin our children's expectations. I wanted to so ignite our children's expectations about having a vibrant relationship with Jesus and being part of a vibrant relationship with a community of faith that, when they grow up, they will choose jobs and make decisions about moves and promotions based on whether or not there is a place like The Orchard in that community. And, in the case where they have no options, they would drive an hour in any direction to find one, or rather than settle for less, start one! I believe Jesus expects nothing less from any of our churches.

I challenged all of us to ruin it for those who think Jesus and his followers have nothing to say, nothing to offer to them. For everyone who hears the word "church" and thinks they just want my money, my time, my talents, my *whatever* for themselves, I wanted us to love them, serve them, invite them, give them, and support them— with no strings attached. So that, when everything inside them is saying, "It can't be true" or "I won't believe it," their souls simply will not be able to agree.

I believe this is Jesus' call to every community of faith that would bear His name. We are all distinct parts of the body and all necessary (See 1 Corinthians 12.4-17). We all must play our distinctive roles, and that comes by discovering, celebrating and even creating our niche in our ministry context as we reach the world for Christ.

It is vital that our churches create a niche where the unchurched in our communities, hear, understand and choose faith. I have a notebook full of collected emails and cards from newly reached people relating to me how much The Orchard means to them. I received this one recently:

Thanks from a 5 year old who was taken by her step-father. Thanks from a 13 year old baby having a baby and 2 more before she was 17. Thanks from a teenage mother who lost 2 children to death in the streets before they or she could know how to get out and save them. Thanks from a mother of 1 who has no knowledge of life but what she learned in the streets, gang banger, drug dealer, and knowing that God (what she knew of him) was that you were loved if you did not OD, go to jail, or get shot (that day). Thanks from a mother who loses her last child to the system for bad decisions, wrong paths, just not caring enough about herself, drugs and not because she didn't love him. Thanks from a twenty something in prison for crimes too sad to mention but having to know you will live with the shame and guilt for ever and ever. Looking in the mirror and seeing only the ones you have hurt and nothing of any good you have done. Thanks from an early thirty something mother who never though to have a child, who still knows nothing of life and the Love of the Lord but keeps hearing people say there is a way to fill that black pit in your insides with other things besides drugs and alcohol. Thanks from a recovering addict, recovering alcoholic for a place that finally, finally, finally she understands, fits in, and does not have to be something she is not to believe that God can love all she is, all she was and all she so desperately wants to be. So for all of the above, from a very lonely unchurched, thanks for a place that is so much of what this woman, mother, recovering addict, and now one who can see a light at the end of what has been a very, very long, very, very dark tunnel. I look forward to many more moving, loving sermons like last Sunday. I cannot again say it enough for myself and for my son. Just wanting to return some of the love I feel when I walk into this wonderful place (used by permission; name withheld).

Thinking different, so that people can hear the good news...that they can be different is what creating a niche is all about.

CHAPTER 4

And a Little Child Shall Lead Them

†══──══†

$\mathcal{N}$o other focus more radically affects your ministry for good or bad as the way you handle people's children. Please stop and read that statement again. Let it soak in. *No other focus more radically affects your ministry for good or bad as the way you handle people's children.*

The sermon and music can be average, and people still give you a second chance if you have taken good care of their children. The late, Dr. Bill Hinson, retired pastor of First United Methodist Church in Houston, Texas said, "People are bringing you their trophy children. And they want to know how you are going to display them, protect them and honor them." (Speech given at The Epworth Institute, August 2004).

Wendy, and I struggled with infertility for almost seven years. We now have two beautiful adopted children. However, when we were going through the heart-wrenching process of trying to become parents we began to recognize what a child-centered culture we live in. Every holiday is centered around and marketed to children. Our society in general expects that married people have children, and if they don't, they will often be asked why they don't. We decided that if and when we had children that we would be more sensitive to families of all shapes, sizes and numbers, eliminating any sense of bias or predisposition toward only families with children.

However, when God entrusted two little lives to us, our perspective radically changed. The principle of *not* being a child-centered family was met with the reality that if you have a child, you are by necessity a child-centered family. Their complete and utter dependence upon you as parents dictates it. Admittedly, some parents take this to the extreme. I remember sitting at a football game behind a particular family watching "Junior" run his parents ragged trying to meet his demands for comfort, food, drinks, bathroom, and souvenirs—and this child was eight or nine years old!

Even the most differentiated parents still have to give an intense amount of focused attention and energy to their children. This principle will never change.

Not long after becoming parents, Wendy and I visited a new church plant while on vacation. Since The Orchard was a startup, we like to visit new churches and encourage the pastor. This particular new church was meeting in a YMCA. We arrived and found friendly people, and they pointed us toward the room they had set up as a nursery. We settled our children and found the worship space. We were there for an hour and while the music and sermon were good and the people friendly, my mind never left my children. During the entire service, I wondered if I should go check on them. Were they all right? Was someone playing with them? Were they in danger? That day gave me insight into the mind of parents who sit in our congregation, and it helped me see that while The Orchard was doing a good job in children's ministries, "good" was not good enough.

Common Problems

We have all heard the tales of the "nurseries from hell." Chipping paint, dark walls in the basement, broken toys and dangerous furniture are not the kind of problems I intend to discuss here. Surely we all have enough "discernment" to know that a bright, clean, safe environment *for every age level* of our children's ministries is crucial.

Further complicating the matter is the number of parents who must put their children in daycare. Today, many children spend significant amounts of time either in daycares or after school programs. The result for many parents is an enormous amount of guilt, frustration and financial burden. Arising from these is a thought process that determines dropping their child at one more childcare facility may be too much; therefore, leaving their children in the nursery or children's ministry program at church ranks as more than simple childcare for many parents. In today's world, churches really do compete with the myriad of emotional struggles and responses that parents face during the week.

Additionally, people want to know that your Children's ministry program isn't simply "babysitting." They require assurance that your church is a transforming and wonderful experience that positively affects their family. How can we make sure this happens?

If we expect parents to bring themselves wholly into the worship service, then we must help ease their minds about how we are caring for their children. Never underestimate the power of words in putting parents at ease. However, never overestimate them either. It takes clear words, thoughtful strategy and concrete action for children's ministry to reach a level of greatness.

Clear Words

At The Orchard, one of the things we always say is, "Both the Sprout Patch and the GrowZone ministries are designed to take really good care of your kids..." This simple assurance statement lets them know that we realize the incredible act of trust a parent makes in sharing their children with us. We take the matter very seriously.

It is also imperative that you constantly communicate with parents about what you will be doing, where in the building you will be going (if relocation is part of your plan), and how you will contact them in case of emergency. One Sunday, Wendy, who is our minister to younger children and families, noticed a mother in tears. The mother had gone to pick up her child after the service but discovered that he was not in the same room where she had left him. She was obviously panicked and very upset. Someone had neglected to tell the mother that her son's age group relocates to a large group room for music and worship near the end of the morning. Wendy took the woman by the arm and assured her that her son was fine, and we were taking good care of him. However, the assurance did not stop there. Wendy then took the mom to her child's room so that she could see for herself.

The communication breakdown of this incident was soothed somewhat by the overarching truth—"we are taking good care of your son." Needless to say, we learned from our mistake.

Thoughtful Strategy

There are two perspectives that guide our thinking about children's ministry at The Orchard. One is called "A Spoonful of Influence." The other, which was pioneered by Northpoint Community Church in Alpharetta, Georgia, is "Partnering with the Family."

The idea for "A Spoonful of Influence" came one Sunday morning when I set up a gallon glass jar to represent the life of an 8 year old in our congregation. I related that in one year this 8 year old has 8,760 hours of time. Of that time, 2,920 hours will be spent sleeping (hopefully!). 1,890 hours will be spent in school; On average 1,460 hours will be spent watching TV or playing video games; 1000 hours will be spent with friends/peers; and 1095 hours eating. After each of these pronouncements, I poured a proportionate amount of water in the jar of his life. Then I announced that those hours accounted for 8,270 hours leaving approximately 490 hours yearly of "free time." I then announced that 104 of those remaining hours will be spent in the Ri-Zoo or the GrowZone. As I let the thought of so few hours of actual impact sink in, I added one spoonful of food coloring to represent those 104 hours. The reaction was palpable. Although a small act in its own right, the impact was great as the whole jar changed color. Similarly, the impression of just one hour of effective children's ministry can change a child's life forever.

It all boils down to is this: Of the 8,760 hours in each year, teachers and helpers in Ri-Zoo get 104 hours maximum with our children. That is 1/84 of their annual time. But those 2 hours per week can color their world. It is the most profound two hours of their week, because what happens there can change their lives. That is impact. One way to look at children's ministry is that we get 104 hours annually to influence a child, and it is imperative that we make the most of it. We must have great atmosphere, interesting curriculum, prepared teachers, and loving greeters. The Holy Spirit can do wonderful, dare we say miraculous, things with 104 hours, especially if we do our part of preparation.

And, yet, the other way to look at Children's ministry is that out of those 8,760 hours each year, we *only* have 104 of them. So, even in a best-case scenario, we don't have a tremendous amount of influence. This perspective is why we adopted Northpoint's "Partnering with the Family" approach. It seeks to draw the parents onto the team who influence their children and shape the ministry's focus. We not only influence the children as much as we can, we help the parents prepare to influence their children by giving them helpful tools and opportunities to talk with their children about faith.

It may seem odd to hold both perspectives: that we *have* 104 hours, but we *only have* 104 hours. But we feel the tension between these two perspectives is the best way to do the most effective job of taking good care of God's special little gifts. How do we do that? The answer is that to a) our clear words and b) our thoughtful strategy we add c) concrete action.

Concrete Action

Every Sunday our birth through five-year-old kids spend their time in *The Sprout Patch*. In The Sprout Patch nurseries, we play Christian lullabies and love on the children.

When a child reaches one year old, we begin to teach them age appropriate scripture verses and songs. By age two, we have added a short lesson to go along with playtime. For ages 3, 4 and 5 we teach a lesson, sing songs, develop a craft and even structure their playtime to reinforce the lesson that we are trying to teach for that day. The plan is very ordered and specific to each age group and developmental stage. At the same time, our kindergarten through fifth graders experience their own high-energy worship service called *The Grow Zone*. The Grow Zone runs concurrent with our adult worship service and is structured as large group to small group format time. The program is divided into Kindergarten through second grade; third and fourth grade; and fifth grade. Each age group participates in active worship that includes singing, body movement and hand motions that get the kids involved right from the start. Then, one of our gifted and trained teachers presents a large group teaching experience that is eventually unpacked within each child's small group with games, discussion and interaction centered on what they just heard. At the end of the hour, these children go home with a craft, a song, and a lesson that they can discuss with their parents.

Just in case families miss The Sprout Patch or The Grow Zone we offer a family worship service called *Ri-Zoo*.

Ri-Zoo (which is the Greek word for "rooted") is an experience patterned after Northpoint Community Church's Kidstuff ministry and targets first through fifth graders. This forty-five minute service, which happens between our two morning services, requires parents to attend with their children. High energy music, theme teaching, and recurring characters who teach a biblical life lesson lend a "kid's theater" feel to this exciting hour. Then, as they leave, families are handed a "God-Time Card" that serves as a discussion guide for the whole family to process what God is teaching them as disciples at every stage of life.

Greatness is...

Jim Collins in his book *Good to Great* writes that good is the enemy of great. Our settling for good children's ministries often keeps our churches from doing something great in children's ministry. We often do many things well, but very few of them with excellence.

My dad used to say, "You can be a jack of all trades and master of none." I am sure that the saying didn't originate with him, but he always lived by it. Great churches live by it too. They decide that they can't and won't try to do everything in children's ministries. They decide that they can't and won't develop so many programs that they are unable to develop or staff any of them well. Instead greatness comes when churches decide to be clear with their words, thoughtful with their strategy and concrete in their actions. Probably no other focus has the opportunity to radically affect your ministry for good or bad as the way you handle people's children. And nothing will affect the way you handle people's children more radically than your commitment to a clear and thoughtful process that leads to effective, life transforming age level ministries.

CHAPTER 5

Know Where You Are, and Are Not

⊹⊱━⊰⊹

In 1997, Wendy and I moved to Kentucky to be part of The Beeson Pastor Program at Asbury Theological Seminary. Under the leadership of Dr. Dale Galloway and Dr. Ellsworth Kalas, we spent the next eleven months traveling across The United States visiting cutting edge churches of every shape, form and denomination. Not all of them were large churches, but all of them were unique churches. The culmination of our year together was a fourteen-day trip to Seoul, South Korea where we visited the world's largest churches. My own denomination's (United Methodist) largest congregation is there, as is the largest church in the world. Worshipping at The Yoido Full Gospel Church, a congregation with 720,000 members (at the time) was an experience I will never forget. And it forever shaped the way I understand and practice leading my own congregation.

You may ask what I could learn from a church in Seoul, Korea that was applicable in Tupelo, Mississippi. One insight was that Yoido has a remarkable Cell Church structure. It shaped the way that we structured our small group ministry to be under the care of lay pastors. But as important as understanding what would "translate" into my culture, was understanding what would not.

I had a similar experience at nearly every church we visited. In fact, if you were to visit The Orchard you would recognize a strong influence from five distinct churches (I mentioned this in an earlier chapter). As much as I learned from each of them that I was able to implement at The Orchard, I also learned many things we should never attempt.

For example, The United Methodist Church of the Resurrection (COR) in Leawood, Kansas is an outstanding congregation. In twelve short years, it has grown from a church plant to a congregation with over 8,000 people worshipping there each weekend. The Senior Pastor, Adam Hamilton, told me that when they were preparing to launch they used a marketing program called Phones-For-You. With Phones-For-You volunteers in your congregation make as many as ten thousand (10,000) phone calls letting people know that you are starting a new congregation and inviting them to attend. The desired outcome is that one-percent of those people called will attend your first worship service. COR worked this marketing strategy with great results. However, that same strategy in Tupelo would have sounded the death knell even before The Orchard began.

One of the most important lessons we have learned in leading our congregations is understanding that everything that works for other churches will not for *your* church. This seems elementary. However, one of the gravest mistakes we see repeatedly are churches who visit Willow Creek Community Church, or Northpoint Community Church, or worse—read their denominational magazine that highlights "It Worked for Us!" and try to do exactly the same thing! It is vitally important that you take advantage of the tremendous learning opportunities at cutting edge churches. But don't forget that you must then translate them to your world.

Coming Home to Your World

Pretending that your church is in Chicago or Atlanta, or Los Angeles when it is really in Tupelo, Petal, New Albany or Oxford is a recipe for disaster. People in Tupelo do not see the world even remotely similar to those in Chicago. They don't even see it similarly to people who live in Atlanta, even though it is at least another southern town. Thinking how your people think is essential to knowing where you are and where you are not, and if you can't think how they think, you better at least understand how they think and strategize accordingly.

When I first moved to Tupelo, I met another church planter who was leading a church that was two-years-old at the time. He was a great guy; he had a passion for the lost in Tupelo; he was a good communicator and an excellent pastor. He had one major impediment—he was from Pennsylvania. He worked harder than anyone I know to understand how the southern mind works, but he had to work at it and that put him at a disadvantage in reaching people.

A close friend and I have often talked of planting a church together, but there is no question of what geographical region of the country we would plant in! We are firmly educated in the southern mindset. To ignore this would put us at a disadvantage!

I cannot stress this enough. Either work to understand the world you live in, or move to the world you want to live in. Leading any church is hard enough without the added difficulty of not understanding, and not being sensitive to the culture in which you live.

Shape to their preferences not yours

Eugene Nida, the father of Christian Anthropology, in his book, *Customs and Culture*, recounts this story:

We are not going to have our wives dress like prostitutes," protested an elder in the Ngbaka church in

47

northern Congo, as he replied to the suggestion made by the missionary that the women should be required to wear blouses to cover their breasts. The church leaders were unanimous in objecting to such a requirement, for in that part of Congo the well-dressed and fully-dressed African women were too often prostitutes, since they alone had the money to spend on attractive garments. Different peoples are in wide disagreement as to the amount or type of clothes required by modesty. (Customs and Cultures, page 1).

Nida suggested that the problem is, "Fully equipped with our own set of values, of which we are largely unconscious, we sally forth in the world and automatically see behavior with glasses colored by our own experience." (Customs and Cultures, page 2)

Too many of us try to shape the natives to our preferences in the Christian faith. Pastors often make a major error this arena of cultural dissection. They design their congregation's ministries or worship service to fulfill their needs rather than reach their target audience. They choose songs/ hymns they like; they dictate dress by the way that they dress or initiate ministries that intrigue them and few others. In United Methodism, our Annual Conference sessions serve as the consummate example of what I mean.

Episcopal and denominational leaders design worship services, choosing hymns, readings and highlighting obscure pet projects which meet the denominational expectation or satisfy their need for pomp and circumstance while the grass roots church member and most pastors find themselves disconnected and bored with the whole service. While this practice at the denominational gatherings is endured because attendance is mandatory, this practice in the church will empty it quickly—because attendance is not!

This does not discount the need for pastors to stretch, educate and lead their congregations to a deeper, richer and fuller experience of God. But often, by the way we plan our worship and understand our context, we have little hope of realizing a deeper, richer, fuller experience anyway. Find out what works—what reaches the mindset and heart of those entrusted to your care—and do it.

Understand your Culture

Webster's defines culture as the social and religious structures and intellectual and artistic manifestations that characterize a society. Nida says, "Culture is all learned behavior which is socially acquired, that is, the material and non material traits which are passed on from one generation to another. They are both transmittable and accumulative, and they are cultural in the sense that they are transmitted by the society, not by genes." (Customs and Cultures, 28).

One of the things we learned by asking the right questions in our context was that a primary reason people didn't get involved in church was that they didn't have time. With both parents working and soccer leagues and ballet and working one or two nights a week, parents didn't feel like they could get involved and participate meaningfully. Understanding this mindset helped us develop our strategy of *Worship Plus 2*.

Most churches in the south identify their committed members as those who "are there every time the doors are open." For most churches this means a family attends Sunday School, Sunday morning worship, youth group, Sunday evening worship, Wednesday night programming and likely at least one other commitment during the week. From the beginning at The Orchard we have asked for a simple commitment of *Worship Plus 2*. We want a commitment for weekly participation in Worship, one Growing Deep Ministry (discipleship) and one Branching Out Ministry (serving). People can't change the world, if they are never in it! Commitment is measured by quality, not quantity of participation. We would rather have people commit significantly to three life changing interactions than superficially to six. Given the precious nature of their time, so would they.

What needs to be understood in this attempt to know where you are and where you are not? Here is a list of fundamental understandings I think are vital to reaching your target group:

- What kind of music do they listen to?
- What is their greatest hope?
- What is their greatest fear?
- What is their greatest need?
- What do they want to do better than their parents did?
- What do they not understand about organized religion?
- What do they not like about organized religion?
- What is the biggest reason they don't attend church regularly?

How do you understand your culture?

One of the easiest ways to understand your culture is to be "from there." I grew up in the area of Mississippi in which I pastor. I can think of no better way to understand the culture in which you live than by having grown up in it. Obviously, not all of us have that advantage or have control over where we live. In lieu of this benefit, consider these insight-giving practices.

- *Use your unique gifts or interests:* I love basketball. I was raised in a coach's house and before being called to full-time ministry prepared in college to coach basketball and teach science. When I first moved to Tupelo, I coached a basketball team in the city league as a way of getting to know kids and parents. I have a friend who planted a church in a gated community in which there are ten golf courses. People move there to play golf in their retirement years. Not much of a golf player before planting a church there, he made learning a priority because of the culture training that happened on the back nine! If you are interested in radio controlled cars or planes, find the RC group in your community. If you like softball, play in a league. If business groups are your interest, join the Rotary, Civitan, or Toastmaster's group of your choice. Use who you are to connect with who they are. Then, spend a lot of time listening and watching.

- *Ask*: Earlier I told you about my friend from Pennsylvania who planted in Tupelo. To his credit, we had lunch regularly and he asked me (someone who had grown up in the area) how to understand what was going on in his circumstance. Find a "native" and take them to lunch regularly. Take them fishing, or to ballgames, or whatever is the cultural event in your community. If possible, contract with them to be your sounding board for ideas and ministries, *before* you invest a lot of time and energy in them. As in school, there are no stupid questions when it comes to understanding the culture in which you live — don't be afraid to ask!

- *Local Hangouts*: Find the local places to eat. Get to know at least one waitress by name and ask her regularly how she is doing. I have learned more by watching a local interact with a friend over breakfast than by any other method of cultural dissection. Find the group of people who best represents those you are reaching, and the group of people who best represents those you need to be reaching and spend some time just hanging out with both of them. By doing so you will learn the cultural "no-no's" and you will also learn the cultural barriers. In Tupelo, a train track runs right through mid-town. People east of the tracks don't come west very often and vice versa. It is not a "wrong side of the tracks/right side of the tracks" mentality. Those tracks just represent the edge of necessary travel to reach all the goods and services (including churches) required for life. Though I did not grow up in Tupelo, I have been around Tupelo all my life, but never knew about this barrier until I began to listen.

- *Read*: Every library has local histories on their shelves. One of the culturally shaping events for Tupelo was the tornado of 1936. The Tornado reorganized the town, picking up one whole subdivision and dumping it in a nearby swamp. The Lee County Library has a number of books about the tragedy and other local histories of Tupelo. Tupelo is also the birthplace of Elvis Presley. What impact do you think this fact has on the musical heritage of the area? It also helps to read books that help you understand how to understand culture. I mentioned my favorite earlier *Customs and Cultures* by Eugene Nida; *Mission and Message* is another great text of his. Don't spend so much time with books that tell you about people groups because even within people groups there are geographical distinctives. But books like Nida's and others help develop the dissection mindset, no matter what culture you are in.

- *Convention and Visitor's Bureau*: The local convention and visitor's bureau or Chamber of Commerce has vital demographic information about your community. They need the information for prospective businesses and industries that are considering moving to the community. They also maintain such vital information to share with families who may be relocating to your town. Most times this information is free.

Conclusion

Understanding where you are doing ministry and where you are not is essential to effectiveness in ministry. If on a mission trip in a non-English speaking country none of us would dream of speaking in English simply because it is our known way of communicating. Yet, many pastors take for granted the culture in which they work every day. The stakes are high, the payoff great—we must learn the language.

CHAPTER 6

Know Who You and Are Not

I am hesitant to write a chapter about identity given the surplus of material that has been written about vision, mission and core values in the last five years. It would, however, be malpractice on my part and certainly untrue to my intent with the book if I did not share, even briefly the importance of congregational identity in this pursuit of Kingdom expansion. It is my opinion that on the journey forward, congregational identity must be established at the onset or no sustained forward movement will take place. None of us would take a trip without a destination in mind, yet we lead our churches on just such a journey when we operate without a clear sense of who we are or where God is calling us. Just to make sure we are using the terms consistently, let me share an illustration that I often share with my congregation to define the distinctives of Vision, Mission and Core Values.

Vision is our intended destination. It is where we will be when we arrive. For example, lets assume Memphis, Tennessee a city about ninety miles northwest of Tupelo is our destination. Mission is our intended route to our destination. To get to Memphis from Tupelo, you can travel

U.S. Highway 78 directly there, or you can travel U.S. 45 to Jackson, Tennessee and then take Interstate 40 over to Memphis. The point is, there are numerous routes you could travel to get to Memphis from Tupelo, but you can't travel them all. You must decide. Let's assume we will take U.S. 78. Core Values are our reason for taking the trip. Let's say we are going to the mall shopping.

Translated for The Orchard, our destination (Vision) is to be devoted to the cultivation of fruit for Christ's Kingdom. When everything we do bears fruit for Christ's Kingdom, we will have "arrived." Our determined route to this destination is by "helping people Grow Deep in the love of Jesus and Branch Out to others with that love." And the reason we are on this journey at all is that:

- *We believe that people matter to Jesus Christ.* Therefore we value all people and extend to them the Love of Christ. John 3:16-17; Luke 10:25-37
- *We believe in changed lives through small groups.* Our own relationship with Jesus Christ is changing us, and we focus on connecting others to Christ the Life-Changer. Involvement in a small group is of primary importance in our relating to Christ and relating to others. Acts 20:20; John 1:35-51; Acts 2:43-47;
- *We believe in Fully Devoted Discipleship.* We are called to live as faithful messengers of God's grace and hope in the world. As disciples, we offer our habits, words and lives as witnesses to our faith in Christ. Matthew 16:21-28; I John 2:6; Romans 12:1-2; Luke 14:26-27
- *We believe in God.* The Father who compassionately cares for his children; The Son who gave his life for the world; the Holy Spirit who empowers us to live as witnesses in this world. Genesis 1:1; John 1:1-5; Acts 2:1-4; Acts 2:17-21

- *We believe in Prayer.* We are a church that lives, moves, and has our being in God. Our life is a life of prayer. Matthew 6:5-15; James 5:16; Matthew 26:41; Luke 5:16; Luke 18:1; Acts 17:28
- *We believe the Bible contains the words of Life.* We commit ourselves to the study of God's Word. Joshua 1:8-9; John 17:17; Hebrews 4:12-13; 2 Timothy 3:16-17
- *We believe in authentic Christian Worship.* Worship that glorifies God and exalts Christ in relevant songs, words, media and movement. Matthew 22:34-40; Psalm 100; Hebrews 13:15-16
- *We believe we are gifted by God.* Each of us is uniquely gifted and we seek to discover and use our gifts with excellence as we serve God and others. I Peter 2:9; I Corinthians 12:4-11, 28; Ephesians 4:11-16; Romans 12:6-8
- *We believe in each other.* Christ has called us to live and serve together. Our commitment to Christ is embodied in our commitment to each other. I Corinthians 12:4-7; I Corinthians 12:14-27; Psalm 133; Ephesians 4:1-13
- *We believe in team ministry.* All Christians are ministers and are called to serve together, learn together, and discover innovative ways to communicate the Gospel to the world. I Peter 2:9; I Corinthians 12:14-27; Ephesians 4:11-12

Congregational Identity?

By clearly identifying your congregation's Vision, Mission and Core

Values you clearly define who you are. Likewise, to avoid defining your Vision, Mission, and Core Values identifies your congregation as wandering. My dad used to say, "Aim at nothing, and you will be sure and hit it." Without a defined vision, you are aiming at nothing. Of course you can let yourself off the hook when it comes to mission and core values

57

because without a desired destination (vision) there is no need for a planned route (mission) or motivation (core values).

However, when a congregation does the hard work of identifying each of these components they can direct their budgeting, energy, mission focus and dreams all in that direction and congregational and missional synergy occurs.

From the very beginning The Orchard's target group was people who did not go to church. We call them the unchurched and the de-churched. Our intentional aim was to reach people who had been burned by church or did not understand church and therefore did not participate in any community of faith. For this reason, our congregation could be generally described as contemporary. The dress is casual; we don't do spoken creeds or recited prayers; the music is by a band, and we very rarely do hymns—to name just a few of the characteristics.

In the beginning, we had a retired pastor who was part of our core group and helped me tremendously in the daily activities of planting a church. Very early on he came to my office and insisted that our worship needed to include some of the traditional components of a United Methodist Worship service, i.e. The Apostle's Creed, The Lord's Prayer, and some traditional hymns. But because of our intended target group, I resisted, because to include those things would have given them an experience that matched their expectations—a church that they didn't understand.

Knowing who we were—devoted to the cultivation of fruit for Christ's Kingdom, let us say "no" to some very good things. Given our call to make a Kingdom difference, we were able to make decisions based on what was right for people who were outside the Kingdom, not based on the preferences of those who were already in it. Let's be honest. Each year some people join your church and some people leave your church. By defining your Vision you get to decide who joins and who leaves.

I have had many occasions to be in Chicago. When my wife and I go there, we rarely rent a car, preferring public transportation as an adventure all its own! On one of our first trips we decided to visit the The Chicago Museum of Science and Industry. On the day we had set aside for the museum we didn't go outside the hotel and get on the first bus that came by. We were careful to make sure we knew where the bus was going before we got on, choosing only to pay the fare and get on board when we knew the bus' destination.

When people know where you are going, how you plan to get there and your motivation for taking the trip, they will be able to decide whether they want to go with you or not. The retired pastor decided that he didn't want to take the trip with us and he has become a valuable asset to a traditional congregation in town and is one of our biggest cheerleaders. He is just one example over the years of people who have visited our church and decided that they didn't want to get on board. But for every person who has decided not to get on board, there have been at least two people who have been looking for our "bus" for their whole lives. I believe this clear identity has been one of the key principles in our rapid growth.

Navigational Tools

Congregational identity is not the only reason for a clearly defined vision, mission and core values. Once established they also serve as vital navigational tools.

How does The Orchard use its vision? On a grand scale we measure ourselves every year. Are we producing more fruit this year than last? If not, why not? Are there some ministries that are consuming resources and not bearing fruit? If we are producing fruit in increasing proportions, what are the areas of growth? This annual evaluation against our ideal helps us take a look at our weaknesses and then to begin to plan for ministries that address them.

For example, when a Generation X focused ministry shut down in our town, we realized how much we had relied on them to reach this cross-section of people in our region. Now, without their presence, our weakness was even more glaring and we are currently working out a ministry plan to establish need-meeting ministries for this target group who is unchurched or de-churched.

How does mission help us navigate in ministry? Usually, a defined mission is a more strategically particular tool than vision. Vision is this big arching umbrella, but Mission is our daily measuring stick, because sometimes "visional fruit" is only seen at a distance or after some time. But we can measure "missional fruit" on a daily basis and it stands as the criteria for beginning and/or continuing specific ministries.

At The Orchard, when we ask in our annual evaluation, "Are there ministries that are consuming resources without bearing fruit?" We are trying to divide ministries into three distinct categories: What ministries do we need to prune? What ministries need fertilizing? And, what ministries need uprooting? We can divide all our ministries rather easily into these three categories by simply asking our mission question. Did this ministry help anyone grow deep in the love of Jesus or branch out to someone else with that love this year? That is either a yes or no answer, and we can then make future decisions about resource allocation accordingly. We do not give energy, financial resources or volunteer effort to areas that do not produce fruit.

There is one important thing to keep in mind. Fruit is not always numeric. We don't simply judge a ministry on whether or not it increased attendance in any given year. But when your vision, mission and core values are all clearly defined then everyone can be honest about fruitfulness, potential for it—or obvious lack of it—because you all want the same thing.

Bill Hybels in his tape series, Defining Moments, points out that, "There are no points for predicting rain, only for building the ark." (Audio Tape, Learning from Big Blue). Hybels highlights that it does us no good to say, here is our destination if we don't do anything to get moving toward it. And it does us no good to have a defined vision if we don't do the hard work of eliminating ministries that are distracting us from moving closer to our destination.

Jesus was the perfect model for this. Laurie Beth Jones in her book, *Jesus, CEO* says, "Pause for a moment and consider the things Jesus did not do. Here is someone endowed with limitless power from on high. He could have done literally anything. Yet he did not build a temple or synagogue. He did not write or distribute books. He did not even heal all the sick people in the world. He did not go down to the grave-yards and raise everyone from the dead. He did not build shopping malls. His mission was very specific. Jesus stuck to his mission. (To do God's Will—to become the sacrifice for our sins.) No less clarity of commitment is demanded from those who would call themselves his Body.

Core Values are the lowest common denominator, but they can be the most effective in setting direction. The Orchard uses its core values to say no to many good ministry opportunities because they do not align themselves with the values our congregation holds deeply.

Practically, The Orchard uses its core values as a final qualifier for considering ministry opportunities. An opportunity may be in line without our vision—it may have potential to bear fruit for Christ's Kingdom. Likewise, it may be in line with our mission—it could have strong potential to help someone grow deep or branch out. However, the opportunity also has to be in line with our core values.

For several years the Boy Scouts approached our congregation about beginning a troop. My answer was always the same: "If we can get a team of leaders who have a passion for that ministry, we would love to start a troop." However, for several years we could get one or two leaders interested in leading a troop, but we have a core value that says, "We believe in team ministry." That means that you need to have at least three people who want to give their passion and energy to something that will bear fruit by helping people grow deep and branch out. I am delighted to report that this past spring we had six men who wanted to give themselves to the ministry of Scouting, and we now have Troop 1516 (Wonder where they came up with that number? John 15:16).

Our core values served us well when planning our first facility too. One of our core values is: We believe life change happens best in small groups. Given that value, we built no adult education space in our building, continuing our belief that small groups should be in homes and likewise saving us lots of money that we could devote to other building and ministry needs.

When a congregation has a clearly defined vision, mission and set of core values, decision making is simplified. The people who want to go in the defined direction are on board and the people who don't aren't. Thus, the only discussions are about how to get where you are going, not where you are going.

But what if...

But what if, the people who aren't on board don't leave. My experience tells me that they will. Anyone not on board that hangs around will eventually be severely outnumbered or incredibly miserable. But you have to be fearless in clinging to your vision, mission and core values. If you, as the pastoral leader don't lead with those elements in mind the congregation and its leaders will question your commitment to them and their commitment to them will waiver.

There will be people who just don't "get it." Let me offer advice that I heard my mentor, Dr. Dale Galloway, give repeatedly. "Build the church you want around the church you have." In Orchard terms, I would encourage you not to give energy or attention to ministries that need to die. And pour all your energy and attention in to building a growing group of people who buy into the vision, mission and core values.

The Visual Element to Vision

It sounds a bit redundant to insist that there is a visual element to vision. What we mean here, however, is that the pastor and leaders have to live out this vision, mission and core values. It does me no good to preach that we are devoted to the cultivation of fruit for Christ's Kingdom if I am not cultivating any fruit myself. Likewise, I better be helping someone Grow Deep and Branch Out and doing the same myself. I better value teams and small groups and believe that all people matter to Jesus (another of our core values). In short no written or articulated set of these components carry the weight of them being lived out in a congregation's leaders, especially the pastor.

Conclusion

Let me offer one last insight about congregational identity and vision, mission and core values. These serve as a vital tool to tell your people and the world who you are as a community of faith. But as importantly, they establish for the unchurched and dechurched what you are not. There can be a significant amount of confusion about "who you are" both by those inside and outside the church. There is one critical way to clear up the confusion for both—working out a clearly defined vision, mission and set of core values.

CHAPTER 7

Preaching that Connects

Few subjects are as sensitive to the pastor as the subject of preaching is. As pastors we may be able to receive constructive criticism with a measure of grace when it comes to almost any other aspect of ministry. However, as has been said, the practice of preaching is the act of tearing off a piece of your soul and giving it to a crowd. When such sacrifice is made and the return is criticism instead of gratefulness, the act can be devastating.

Numerous books have been written on the art of preaching, and I do not propose to write a treatise on preaching practice in this chapter. Instead, near the end of this chapter, I will suggest some of the best resources (in my opinion obviously) on the difficult matter. What I intend to delineate instead is the need for practical, clear communication of the Gospel and some of the common pitfalls to doing so.

I had some phenomenal instruction on preaching in seminary. I count myself as blessed to have been taught several great preachers during my years of study—Dr. Donald Demaray, Dr. Ellsworth Kalas, and Dr. Dennis Kinlaw—all contributed to my understanding the weightiness of the craft.

The wonderful instruction of these pastors were tempered by the fact that they had indeed pastored churches and been called upon to serve the Bread of Life to a congregation week in and week out. Seminary professors who suggest that you should spend one hour of preparation for every minute you expect to speak are horribly out of touch with the daily realities of pastoring a church.

Many seminaries do a great job of helping you cognitively understand the preaching task. However, the church is the entity that will demand you also bring practicality to the task. This practicality is not only required in our preparation, but also in delivery and content as well.

Practical Preparation

Everyone who feels gifted to preach or enjoys the act of preaching will tell you that the most difficult part is preparation. The tension between seminary expectations and daily realities of ministry, the hard work of preparing sermons often gets squeezed to the edges of ministry. After all you can say, "no" to sermon prep, but can you really say, "no" to the member of your church who, "just needs a few minutes of your time?" Protected time in which to think, study, and pray is essential in the demanding routine of leading a church. It doesn't matter how you protect time to prepare the weekly sermon, it is however, necessary that you protect time.

I work best in large blocks of time. So I guard one entire day for sermon preparation. Except in emergencies, I see no one, return no phone calls, and take no appointments until the sermon is done. I often tell friends I take the "application" approach to sermon preparation. I apply the seat of my pants to the seat of my chair until it is done. This approach will not work for everyone, but it suits my personal work style the best.

The other part of preparation that is essential is deciding what is important to bring to the table for preparation. For example, I don't spend a lot of time reading commentaries on the text I am examining for a sermon. I restrict myself to primarily one or two outside interpreters. I do so, because I know that as a pastor my time is limited, and by choosing one or at most two well chosen voices I am gathering the most important background on the text at hand. In addition, I only read what is necessary to the interpretation of the text. If the geography of the land in which my passage takes place is not important to my message, I do not spend time reading about the geography of the land. A case in point: When Peter made his historic confession of who Jesus was, "You are the Christ, the Son of the living God." (Matthew 16), the text tells us that the disciples and Jesus were on their way to Caesarea Philippi. This fact is really of little consequence in interpreting the text for my people, so I do not spend time tracking down all the details about Caesarea Philippi.

Equally important to what you will communicate is *how* you communicate. Many pastors spend the majority of their time thinking about what to communicate. However, I advocate spending an equal amount of time on how you will make the truth to be communicated digestible to those who will receive it. For that reason, practical preparation time should include your story files, the newspaper, a healthy understanding of current events and a thorough mental catalog of human experiences and personal connection points. Practical preparation demands that you spend as much time thinking about how you will communicate a truth as you do deciding what truth a text asks you to communicate.

In most cases, as pastors, our time is limited for sermon preparation. Knowing how to use that time is essential to bringing a well-crafted, relevant message to the people on Sunday.

Practical Delivery

In their book *The Leader's Voice*, Clarke and Crossland propose that the most effective communicators use three essential channels to convey their message: Factual, Emotional, and Symbolic.

What we communicate has to be anchored in the facts. For the preacher this is biblical truth. But as Clarke and Crossland add, "Emotions are the wattage of communication. As a leader you must know and articulate constituent's important but unspoken feelings. Constituents (Congregants) constantly scan the emotional channel, tuning in to stations that inspire, encourage and engage.

The most obvious component of Clarke and Crossland's assertion to the preacher should be the use of symbols in speaking. Is there any more profound symbol than Jesus taking bread, breaking it, and saying, "this is my body" or taking the cup and saying, "this is my blood"? This was not the only symbol Jesus used in teaching. In fact every parable Jesus uttered was an exercise in the use of symbols to communicate.

Paul, was no stranger to symbols either. His writing is littered with images of runners, and races, and clouds of witnesses. There is also plenty of evidence that he used symbols of the culture to communicate new facts to his crowds (see Acts 17:16-32).

The evidence of Scripture reveals that Jesus, the master communicator, proves the most effective communicators use three essential channels to convey their message: Factual, Emotional, and Symbolic.

Facts

The preacher must anchor the sermon in Biblical truth. The temptation today is to listen more to the voices of Dr. Phil, Oprah, Freud, Jung, or the Founding Fathers than to listen to the living word of God. Surely the preacher must bring complimentary voices to the conversation, but the core of that conversation must be driven by the immutable word of God. As clearly as I know how, let me articulate this fact: Sermons must begin with, be saturated with, and conclude with biblical truth.

This does not prohibit a preacher from preaching topically. However, to do so, they must find the text that addresses their topic and commit themselves to say what the text says. The temptation is to say what we want to say (or what psychology says) and then find texts to support those claims. To combat this temptation, focus on a single scriptural passage instead of trying to communicate everything the Bible says on one particular subject. Don't be afraid to support your central text with other biblical examples when helpful or insightful, but don't overwhelm your people with so many texts that the message of the central text gets lost. More importantly, don't use your text for a launching pad for your own personal opinions while ignoring the text, context and meaning of the passage of Scripture. The people who gather to worship at your place on any given Sunday can access psychology and secular opinions multiple times daily through any number of communication mediums. Regrettably, most will only receive biblical truth once or twice a week through a relatively few number of mediums. As the preacher, you must take advantage of the opportunity presented to you, at the appointed preaching/teaching hour, to serve them a steady diet of biblical truth.

Emotions

Sermons that do not impassion us about some aspect of the Christian life are not sermons at all. A sermon which touches only the cognitive sectors of our lives inform us but leave us without the motivation to make any real changes. The preacher that calls their congregants to the "higher calling" that Paul refers to must involve their hearts.

It was no accident that the great preachers of the reformation called on the emotions of the people to whom they preached and the emotions of the preachers they directed. When John Wesley said, "Give me one hundred preachers who fear nothing but sin and desire nothing but God, and I care not a straw whether they be clergymen or laymen, such alone will shake the gates of hell and set up the kingdom of God upon the earth." He was appealing to the emotions of those preachers. When John Calvin preached his infamous "Sinners in the hands of an angry God" emotions were at the heart of the message, even if that emotion was fear! Furthermore, Wesley's response to an inquirer about how attracted such large crowds to hear him preach was, "I set John Wesley on fire and people come to watch him burn."

The faithful preacher of the word, not only involves the emotions of those who gather, but he/she begins by engaging his/her own emotions in delivering a passionate message.

Symbols

On one wall in our office suite hang twenty pictures. Each one represents one-thousand people in my town who do not have a personal relationship with Jesus or a connection to a community of faith. Those faces serve as a powerful symbol to remind me of the task at hand. It is easy for the number "twenty-thousand" to become impersonal and detached. However, it is much harder to ignore twenty-thousand faces. Recently when I preached our annual vision, mission, and core values series, I posted those twenty faces on stage so that others could see them. They serve as a powerful symbol reminding people of The Orchard why we exist.

When both Jesus and Paul, the two most prominent voices of the New Testament, spoke they immersed their listeners in symbols. One can hardly turn a page of the Gospels that Jesus does not use the ordinary to communicate the extraordinary. Paul was no less dependent on symbols. In

Acts he confronts the Areopagus by using their own statue to an unknown God (17:16-31); in Romans we are all one body (12:3-5); in 1 Corinthians he reminds them that in a race they should run in a way to obtain the prize (9:24); in 2 Corinthians we are a fragrance present by Christ to God (2:15) and a perishable container that holds a treasure (4:7); in Galatians we are heirs with Christ (3:29); in Ephesians, Paul prays that the Ephesians would put on the whole armor of God (6:10-18); in Philippians Paul strains to reach the end of the race and receive the prize (3:14); in Colossians he instructs them to "let their roots grow down into [Jesus] and draw up nourishment from him…" (2:7); in Thessalonians, he warns them that the day of the Lord will come like a thief in the night." (1 Thessalonians 5:2); in Timothy he says that he has fought the good fight and finished the race…(4:7). And this is just a cursory glance at Paul's writing!

Symbols make the obscure clear, the vague concrete, and the boring memorable. I never will forget what I consider the most powerful use of symbols in all my years of preaching. I was preaching on the need to serve as part of our discipleship. Jesus called us to give ourselves away and I wanted to drive home this point. At the beginning of the sermon, I began to recount for the congregation the "spoonful of influence" perspective that I shared with you in Chapter 4. I carefully detailed how an 8 year old boy uses one year of his time and pointed out how little of that time The Orchard has access to. Then I turned up the impact of the symbol by adding: "But that 8 year old only receives that impact if someone volunteers to teach. That much is obvious right! But there is more to this story." That 8 year old needs the teacher but he also needs; the parking ministry who helps them find a space at the 10:30 service or if they happen to come to the 8:30 service, helps them get out of the parking lot without so much trouble that aggravation sets in; the man and woman who give 2 hours per week to make the coffee, because without the coffee dad is not going to get up to bring him; the woman who gives 2 hours per week to pick up and set out the donut holes because if mom has to fix breakfast before they go out the door, they might not get out the door; the Bridgebuilder ministry that gives 2 hours each week that greets his family and tries to make them feel welcome because they are relatively new at The Orchard and are a little intimidated by the crowd. They greet them with a smiling face and hand them a worship flyer so that they don't miss the children's lock-in on Friday night where he will make good friends that will influence him for Jesus and Jesus' way someday; the ladies who give 2 hours per week to take care of his little sister in the nursery so that mom and dad who have been awake most of the night with her, get a break; the men who give two hours per week to teach his little brother in the 3 year old class so that mom and dad feel like there is something for everyone and that they are not just dropping his little brother off in daycare like they have to do the rest of the week because they both have to work; the youth volunteers who volunteer 3-5 hours a week who connect with his older sister in a way that makes her want to be here on Sunday morning so that she will also come back on Sunday night; the musicians who volunteer and practice 2 or 3 hours during the week so that they can present with excellence worship music for 2 hours on Sunday morning that stirs dad's heart even if he doesn't understand all that the preacher says; the media team men and women who give 2 hours each week to run the TV cameras, adjust the sound and lights and run the computer so that his mom and dad can see, hear, and read the lyrics to the songs; the janitorial team who gives 2 hours each week to go behind each service cleaning up cups and paper and bulletins so that the guest his family is bringing this morning has a good first impression; the volunteer who serves 2 hours each week at the information desk to help mom find a CD to share with a friend who is going through a difficult time, but she doesn't know what to say, but she remembers a sermon from several weeks back on just the right subject and now she wants a copy to share with her as a means of encouragement."

As I listed each one of these volunteer areas a person from the congregation representing that ministry came forward and added one tablespoon food coloring to the jar. They then took their place standing behind me on stage in a line. Then pointing to the jar and the volunteers I closed the deal by saying, "All that for one 8 year old boy..." and asking, "When you consider that large scale effort you might ask "is it worth it?" Let me answer that with another question...what if the 8 year old was your son? What if he were your grandson, or nephew? Would it be worth it then?" It was an image our people have never forgotten.

The use of symbols is essential in the communication of the Gospel. It always has been, it is now, and in this visual age more than ever.

Practical Content

I received my first preaching instruction in what United Methodism calls Local Pastor's Licensing School. I don't remember very much about the experience. However, I did learn the single most important question to apply to my preaching: "So what?" My preaching instructor taught us to ask "so what?" at the end of our sermon so that we might keep in mind that if what we just said is not relevant to anyone we should not bother preaching it. Preaching that does not help people interpret their lives in light of the gospel is wasted.

Abraham Lincoln was once engaged leaving a church service by an enthusiastic believer who asked, "Wasn't that a great sermon, Mr. President?" Lincoln is said to have responded, "It wasn't great because it didn't ask me to do anything great."

For many years I have carried an unspoken template in my mind for a great sermon. Recently a mentor of mine asked me to write it down. For me a great sermon must first and foremost have at Scripture at its core. Secondly, a great sermon must ask me to do something great (the "so what?" question) and Finally, it must give me the hope that by relying on God I can indeed do that something great (the *Good* News).

Great sermons occur at the intersection of Scripture and life. Even David recognized the reason for "hiding God's word in his heart" was so that "he might not sin against him." I fear too many sermons are unclear in their purpose and as Charles Swindoll has said, "A mist in the pulpit creates a fog in the pew."

Decide what the intent of your sermon is and navigate toward the achievement of that end. Develop a template for a great sermon or use mine to evaluate if all the necessary components are present, and look for the intersection between life and Scripture.

Preaching does not have to be complex to be profound. The word we speak is a living word, and if we speak it faithfully then we are promised it will not return void.

Recommended Books on Preaching
- Introduction to Homiletics by Don Demaray
- Biblical Preaching by Haddon Robinson
- Marketplace Preaching by Calvin Miller
- Inductive Preaching by Ralph and Gregg Lewis
- Preaching by Fred B. Craddock

CHAPTER 8

Free Stuff Draws a Crowd

*M*y father-in-law has every tool known to mankind. He is a master electrician and carpenter. For his retirement enjoyment, he built his own house. We spend every Christmas Day at his house doing all the traditional Christmas festivities—eating, opening presents, eating, visiting with friends, eating, napping, eating…well you get the picture. On the day after Christmas we also take part in a sacred tradition—the after Christmas sales. There is something I find very interesting about this shopping tradition, however. My father in law visits all the hardware and tool stores to take advantage of their buy one/get one free sales. It amazes me that he would buy one of what he already has so he can get a second (or third depending on how you look at it) one of what he already has for free.

Why does he participate in such madness? The same reason that all of humanity does—free stuff—even if we don't need it—is too good to pass up.

Conspiracy of Kindness

My exposure to this principle as related to the church happened in a small group gathering with Steve Sjogren then pastor of The Cincinnati Vineyard Church. That meeting and his book *A Conspiracy of Kindness* changed forever the way I, and consequently The Orchard looks at outreach in our community.

Sjogren personally begin to do radical acts of service in the Cincinnati community as a way to communicate God's love in a practical way. What happened was that people were attracted to God through these radical acts (Steve's intent) and attracted to The Cincinnati Vineyard (a pleasant byproduct). Steve and The Vineyard became known for toilet cleaning in public restrooms, feeding meters of parked cars, raking yards and shoveling snow for complete strangers, and even for changing light bulbs for senior adults who couldn't reach some of the bulbs themselves.

His aforementioned book, tells the story, but also lists hundreds of kindness project ideas that any local church can organize in their own communities. I recommend it highly!

Right from the start The Orchard began to organize community kindness projects as a way to startle people with the startling love of God. I use the word startle because that is exactly the reaction of people when people who live in a "nothing is free" society receive something for free—as an expression of God's love.

The first reaction of a startled someone is a "did I misunderstand you?" look; the second reaction is to ask, "Why?" And there is the open door to introduce them to the God who offers them his love just as freely.

Sjogren's book is the complete "how to" and "why to" manual on kindness projects. However, it was never meant to be comprehensive. In fact, its best use is to get you thinking about what might work in your context. At The Orchard a few things that have worked really well have been:

- *Free Soft Drinks:* Coke and Pepsi both have portable serving trailers for outdoor events. In our community you can rent either of these for about $200, and that includes the soft drink and serving cups. With their permission, we set up our trailer outside our town's largest retailer and gave away free drinks all day. In the August heat, we got a little sunburned, but everyone wanted something to drink—even when initially they thought we were selling drinks to raise money. Imagine their surprise!

- *Christmas Wrapping*: We asked for and received permission from our local Books-A-Million to wrap books people bought for Christmas gifts. Many people buy books, and the hassle of wrapping, or the inability to wrap (as is my case) makes this a welcome service. For the cost of a little tape, ribbon and wrapping paper we wrapped people's gifts for free and made a lasting impression for God.

- *Seed Packet Give-Away*: Every year on Easter weekend we stand outside the entrance of Lowe's Home Improvement Warehouse and hand out seed packets. In Mississippi, Easter is the time of year when the weather is warming up and people, after a winter of being stuck inside, want to get out and work in the yard. A local printer prints our logo and worship times right on the seed packet. We simply hand one to each customer and say, "Happy Easter from The Orchard."

- *Balloons*: Want to make an impression with the children of your community? Give away balloons. Our town has several community wide events each year: Fourth of July Fireworks, The semi-annual Air Show, and A Town Festival (ours is called Gum Tree Festival). At each of those community wide events we hand out free helium filled balloons with our logo on them to every child that asks. Sometimes we are able to pass through the crowd and hand them out. Sometimes we have to set up a booth, but if you have a balloon booth, believe me, the children will find you!

- *Easter Egg Hunt*: Up until a few years ago our community hosted a city wide Easter Egg Hunt at the park. For numerous reasons they are no longer able to host that event. Our church voluntarily took over the Easter Egg hunt with the city's blessing. It gives us the opportunity to reach thousands who bring their kids out to the park, who might resist bringing their kids to church. If your church does not have the place to host just such an event, contact the city, and see if your church might put on the event for them. Give them equal sponsorship and recognition. Most government officials would welcome the added recognition!

- *Calendars*: As the year draws to a close each December, everybody needs a calendar for the New Year. One year, we ordered calendars with our logo and worship times printed on them. Standing outside the local grocery stores, where everyone is headed for their last minute Christmas food shopping is great place to give people who have been shopping for gifts a free gift that they can use all year long!

- *Feed The Hungry*: During the first four years of The Orchard's existence, immediately following our Sunday morning Thanksgiving service, we ate a potluck Thanksgiving meal together. As our church grew, we eventually ran out of room for everyone to eat together, and then someone had a brilliant (Spirit-inspired) idea—instead of feeding ourselves—why not feed others. So for the past three years we have cooked meals, put them in take-out trays and delivered them to elderly shut-ins, impoverished neighborhoods and households whose names have been given to us by The Salvation Army and the local Meals-On-Wheels program.

- *Fall Festival*: One event is just too big to take on the road. With every other kindness project we undertake we move out into the community to serve, but our fall festival is located on site. Each year on the Sunday afternoon nearest Halloween we rent gigantic inflatable games, perform live music (secular), and provide countless games, events and activities for the community—all for free. A good time is had by everyone who attends; children have a safe place to "trick or treat" in their costumes and the adults get to "come and see" that there are some fairly normal people that go to church! No kindness project that we do reaches more people each year than this event. In a culture that puts on fall festivals as fundraisers, we prefer to put them on as *fun* raisers. After all, the kingdom of God is a party!

<u>Anyone Can Do This</u>

I have given you a few ideas that have worked best for us. I have friends all over the country who have initiated outstanding kindness projects in their own community—giving out tape for wrapping at Christmas, handing out stamps at the post office on tax return day, and handing out bottles of water at local races are just a few of the amazing ideas that get carried out in the name of Jesus.

It is important to note that a*nyone* can do these projects. Some of our attendees who are shy jump at the chance to hand out seed packets and say "Happy Easter." It is an easy way to introduce people to serving, and usually after serving and having a great experience they expand their serving. The ease of these projects also builds the serving confidence of individuals by giving them a "success in serving" story. Families can serve together. Children can be involved. Both those being served and those serving are impacted.

I could go on about the impact of giving away free stuff. But, nothing will convince you of the possibilities of kindness projects like that person who gives their life to Christ because someone introduced them to his free love by giving them something as seemingly insignificant as a soft drink for free. By investing a small amount of money needed to do almost any "free stuff" project, you can profoundly affect those in your church and those who don't go to the church at all. People who serve together grow closer to one another, people who are served get a little taste of the free love of God, and your church gets the reputation in the community as one who will do strange stuff—like give away free stuff—to reach people for Christ.

Free stuff draws a crowd. And, if giving stuff away for free draws people to the free love of God so that they may indeed be free—then any cost we incur is worth it!

CHAPTER 9

Jack of All Trades and Master of None

In 1984, the high school basketball team I played on finished the season with two wins and twenty-seven losses. My high school baseball team finished with four wins and eleven losses. The track team placed third in one meet that year and there were only three teams in our division at that meet. Needless to say it was a dismal year for sports during my freshman year of high school. The coach, who happened to coach all three sports, resigned at the end of the school year and my dad was hired as the new coach. The first day on the job my dad discontinued the track program by this reasoning: You can be a jack-of-all-trades and a master of none.

I had heard my dad use that phrase hundreds of times before, but not until that day did the meaning really sink in. You can try to do everything and end up doing it in a mediocre way. Or, you can do a few things and do them very well. My dad's philosophy about coaching carried over into my philosophy about ministry. It is my belief that most churches try to do too many ministries, programs, emphases, and events to do all (or any) of them well. In the end, they end up being a "jack of all trades, but a master of none."

Attending the 2002 Catalyst Conference in Atlanta further convinced me of this point. Andy Stanley, the pastor of Northpoint Community Church in Alpharetta, Georgia, talked about how he taught himself to juggle and showed how he was very proficient at juggling three balls. However, he added, he was not as proficient at juggling four balls and was rarely able to juggle five or more balls well.

There are a defined number of ministry emphases that any church can excel at keeping in the air and the church that tries to juggle more rarely does so well.

The Magic Number

I am sorry to disappoint those of you who are expecting an exact number of ministry emphases for your church in this section. I believe the number varies slightly with each community of faith but that, generally, between three and five emphases are enough for any congregation. Now, each of the emphases may have numerous ministries under them, but too many emphases mean too many ministries, which usually equals ineffectiveness in both.

At The Orchard, we focus on three emphases. All our ministries are organized around these three: Worship, Growing Deep, and Branching Out. We define this as our strategy of Worship Plus 2. We want everybody in Worship; we want them involved in one ministry that is helping them grow deep in the love of Jesus and involved in one ministry that is helping them branch out to others with the love of Jesus. Once you have defined the areas of emphasis then you can begin the difficult process of deciding which of your ministries move you toward your goal and which are simply distractions (see the chapter...knowing who you are and who you are not). Don't be deceived. It can be just as difficult to decide which ministries are most effectively moving you toward the realization of your emphases as it is determining the emphases.

An Early Mistake

From the beginning, The Orchard was determined to be a church of small groups, not just a church with small groups. This small group approach is one of our core values and the main ministry for helping people grow deep.

While we were clear about the emphases we began several ministries that distracted us from the major tool for accomplishing growing deep.

We launched on December 6, 1998 and by early April of 1999, we already had in place three significant growing deep ministries. Two of these ministries seemed vibrant if you looked at the attendance, but one of them was struggling. Interestingly enough the one that was struggling was the one that we had determined from the beginning would be our core growing deep ministry—small groups.

From the inception of The Orchard, we decided that we would not be a Sunday School Church opting instead for a Small Group driven discipleship ministry. But when a growing number of people were looking for a discipling experience we created a ministry called Prep Time. Prep time met on Sunday mornings, the hour before worship and we had classes for all age groups—sounds alarmingly similar to Sunday School doesn't it? Sunday School is exactly what we had. It smelled like Sunday School, looked like Sunday School, felt like Sunday School but it wasn't Sunday School because we didn't call it Sunday School. Self-deception is the cruelest kind.

About the same time, we launched a short-term class emphasis on Wednesday nights called G.R.O.W. (Get Revived on Wednesdays). We ordered Pizzas and after dinner, I usually taught a book of the Bible and someone else would teach a "how to" class and we had an interactive curriculum we used with children.

Both Prep Time and G.R.O.W attracted about 150 people weekly. The problem was that both groups were the same 150 Orchard attenders. Complicating matters further was the fact that we had grown to nearly five-hundred in worship and only had about 80 people in small groups. You can understand my concern! A church so heavily built on worship without sustained spiritual growth beyond Sunday morning gatherings is in danger of imploding or stagnation.

The whole staff was aware of the issue, but the turning point came in 2000, when two of my staff members returned from a conference passionate not only about remembering *why* The Orchard was called to a specific ministry, but also *what* we were uniquely called to do. It was clear that we had moved away from our core convictions and if we were ever going to move back—now was the time.

One month later, in May, I gathered all the Prep Time Adults together in one room and told them that Prep Time and G.R.O.W., which usually took a break in the summer, would not be restarted when we gathered again in the fall. In addition, I announced that the only adult growing deep opportunity would be provided in small groups. We would continue to provide a children's ministry on Wednesday nights for grade school children, but youth and adults would be in small groups.

Needless to say this was not one of my finer leadership moments! I clearly cast the vision for the need for the change. I noted that Prep Time and G.R.O.W discipled the same 150 people each week while we currently ignored the other 350 people in our community who were telling us that they would not or could not be discipled in either of those two ways. No one argued with my premise; but a large group, including some of our core group members, was very upset. I did not spend enough time anticipating their concerns about the ministry change, and therefore I couldn't help soothe those concerns. In hindsight I would have spent more time with my influencers, teachers and leaders making sure they understood why the change was necessary and having them help me preach that message thoroughly throughout the congregation.

The whole experience taught me two valuable lessons. One—it is easier to never birth something than it is to kill it. The moment a ministry is born it becomes somebody's baby. In fact, it may become several people's baby and putting a ministry to death is a personal, emotional event for those involved. So be very careful what you help birth! Second—never, never, never, never allow a ministry to be birthed that detracts from what you have determined the core ministries of your church to be. Our small groups have flourished during the years since we eliminated competing ministries—but we are noticeably behind the growth curve in small groups because of that two year impediment.

Competition

I want to be clear that I am not saying that you must eliminate Sunday School or Wednesday night programming. I am saying you have to eliminate *any* distractions from what you have determined to be your core ministries. Churches cannot execute three large-scale discipleship emphases at one time and do all of them with excellence.

It was easy for us to determine which of the ministries to eliminate based on our core value that stated, "We believe life change happens best in small groups." That being a deeply held belief we had to eliminate anything that distracted us from small groups.

Eliminating competition for your core ministry is necessary because, given all the options in any particular ministry category (i.e. Growing Deep/Discipleship) people will always choose the most convenient one even if it is the least effective or has the least impact on their lives. In our case, Prep Time was convenient. People were already up, already dressed and on their way to church. Why not provide something for discipleship while they were already there? The reason for us was that Prep Time addressed the study component of discipleship and somewhat addressed the community component, but left out the other big three components of discipleship for us: outreach, shepherding and leadership development. It was difficult for all of those components to be addressed in an hour-long gathering in which people were hurrying in, settling their children, grabbing a cup of coffee and trying to get the lesson finished before worship started. The community component was reduced to a quick, "how was your week?" between gulps of coffee as the leader was beginning the class.

G.R.O.W. was no less convenient. We provided supper at a minimal cost, and plenty of head knowledge. Most people could fill their stomach and their heads and leave having never addressed four of the five essential components regarding discipleship as we define it.

Small groups, meeting at an alternative time, off-site allowed us to address all five components of discipleship as we defined it. Though it was not the most convenient when the other two ministries were available, the people who have immersed themselves in small group life would now never settle for less.

Can't Pick Up Anything Else until...

This is not to say that our Growing Deep ministries will never involve more than small groups. However, we will never start anything that detracts from them. We have numerous ideas in addition to small groups for helping people grow deep: mentoring relationships, recovery groups, weekend seminars, and online learning communities. Nevertheless, we will only start those as they contribute to small group ministries and we will only start them as small group ministries grow stronger and gain enough momentum that we can devote attention to these new ministries without short-changing the energy or attention needed for small groups to flourish. Our rule is that if our plate is full, we can't pick up anything else until we have cleaned our plate.

New ministries that are launched should stand up to rigorous questioning: Is this ministry in line with our vision, mission and core values? Does it distract us from our core ministries or detract from them in any way? Do we feel this ministry should be added to our cadre of ministries or should it replace one? Anytime you add a "trade", you should ask is there a "trade" we should put down. Doing a few things very well outproduces doing many things with mediocrity.

Over-meeting Your People

There is a personal side of this narrowing of options too. Families who have been in church for most of their lives often feel a need to be there "every time the doors are open." If you have Sunday School, morning worship, Sunday evening, Wednesday evening and small groups. They spend time with the church community potentially five different times each week. With already hectic schedules, the church begins to contribute to the fracturing of the family instead of the healing of it. I know very few, if any, families with children who can make the commitment to be at church five times a week and be engaged all five times.

Let's face it. Between work, soccer games, birthday parties, recreation, family visits, and school we don't need five other events on our schedule each week. What we need (or can truly tolerate) is two, maybe three quality commitments that help us get a grip on the rest.

In my opinion, those who feel the need to be there every time the doors are open shouldn't be there that often, and those who are just returning to church won't be there that often. Ultimately, when we meet that many times weekly, the church is not able to present its best (jack of all trades and master of none) and the people who attend are not at their best (most receptive).

Worship Plus Two

With that in mind, The Orchard proposed a strategy for growth that we believe maintains a healthy balance. We call it Worship Plus Two. We want everyone who calls The Orchard their home to be involved in weekly worship and weekly in Growing Deep (Discipleship) and weekly in Branching Out (Serving). We don't want you involved in more than that because we believe if you will commit to quality involvement in those quality opportunities you will be changed more than if you committed to five mediocre ones.

The other motivating force behind this strategy is that if we expect God's community to transform the surrounding community, we have to allow them time to be part of it. If our people gather in three quality transforming or challenging opportunities each week instead of being there every time the doors are open, then they are not only transformed, but have time to become transformers in the world in which they live. And that is the trade Jesus called us to master (Matthew 28:19-20).

Conclusion

Laurie Beth Jones in her powerful book, *Jesus CEO* says it well, "Pause for a moment and consider the things Jesus did not do. Here is someone endowed with limitless power from on high. He could have done literally anything. Yet he did not build a temple or synagogue. He did not write or distribute books. He did not even heal all the sick people in the world. He did not go down to the graveyards and raise everyone from the dead. He did not build shopping malls. His mission was very specific. Jesus stuck to his mission."

What is on your church's plate that is distracting you from doing ministry with excellence? What is the specific missional task that Jesus has given your church; and what is keeping you from accomplishing it? Jesus stayed focused and so must the communities of faith that bear his name.

CHAPTER 10

Collaborative Pastoring

✛⸺✛

*G*eoffrey Chaucer's *Canterbury Tales* tells the story of a collection of people who are on a journey together. Some of them are friends, some of them merely sojourners, but they are all on the trip together. Along the way, they each tell a story to pass the time and each becomes appreciated for the individual journey they are on. They don't all become close friends or even companions, but they begin to appreciate one another simply because they are on a shared journey.

Ministry is not unlike Chaucer's tale. Over the course of sixteen years in ministry, I have met hundreds if not thousands of other ministers. Most of them are merely sojourners who stories I have come to appreciate simply because we are on a shared journey. There are a few who have become dear friends and companions along the way, without which I am not sure I could have taken this trip at all.

One of the absolutely essential pieces of this ministry puzzle is finding friends to share the journey with. This may be even more important if the ministry you lead or the minister you are has an unusually unique thumbprint.

I regularly meet with three other pastors who live in other cities. The affinity that I share with this group of pastors is somewhat influenced by the uniqueness of our ministries. For starters, three of the four started churches and there is an interesting brotherhood between pastors who begin churches. All four of us lead young (in congregational age) congregations and all of us are within a four-hour drive of a central location where we meet. We are all about the same age and same station in life regarding family. Three of us went to the same seminary and two of us were ordained by the same judicatory (annual conference for United Methodists). However, the factor that ties us most strongly together is our absolute passion for reaching people for Christ and seeing their lives transformed. Along with this comes our willingness to go to great lengths and risk in great measure to see this passion realized.

Each of our ministries are unique in their own way, but all of them are unique in the denominational regions in which we serve. Now you might think that the reason we get together is to share ideas, or encourage one another, or problem solve, or laugh or to just relax. All of those things happen anytime and every time we get together. But the primary reason we get together on a regular basis is to look each other in the eye and tell one another, "You are not crazy."

This conversation is ritualized. We don't beat around the bush, we don't mix words. Before any of our gatherings break up, we look each other in the eye and affirm each other with, "You are not crazy." Who knows maybe we are; but at least we are all crazy together! This custom is our way of saying, "You are not crazy to risk, dream, work, pray, bleed, sweat and cry for the kingdom of Christ to be realized on earth."

Planting a church and establishing a non-traditional ministry is the hardest ministry task I have ever put my hand to. There have been plenty of naysayers and advice-givers along the way. My wife and I even had someone pray over us, "Lord, prepare this couple for failure" as we began to plant The Orchard! Given all the challenges and pressures, I don't know if I could have made it if I hadn't had a group of friends who continually told me "You are not crazy."

Ministry is hard. Planting a church, leading a church, or trying to revive a church all register very high on the pressure gauge of a pastor. The only way anyone can survive long-term is in a community of pastors or friends.

Non-Essential Connections

Most of you may be thinking that you already have a connection. Honestly, most pastors do. However, the first place most of us look for our connection is in a denomination. Let me assure you that you can find a supportive connection within the denomination in which you serve. However, you are just as likely to find one outside your denomination as you are inside it.

For this reason, I believe that connections in general fall into non-essential and essential connections. We can live without the non-essential connections—hence the name. It is not just being in a connection per se that is important. It is the quality and nature of that connection that is vital.

Non-essential connections include connections such as:

- Committees that you sit on that take energy from you rather than energize you.
- Community boards
- Civic groups
- Ministerial Associations
- Regional Denominational gatherings (districts and clusters for United Methodists)

All of these may serve some function, but in general, they are non-essential to your overall spiritual sanity.

When looking for a connection it is not essential that you find *someone who shares your ideas about ministry.* Maybe their ideas are just as off the wall as your ideas they just happen to be off the wall in another direction! I have found that what is important is that you find a connection that shares a similar view on risk that you do. For example, someone whose risk threshold is set at "whatever it takes to win someone to Jesus" will find little support or connection to someone who's risk threshold is "whatever it takes as long as it doesn't upset anyone in the denomination." You may find a connection with someone who has a very different approach to ministry than you. It is not essential that they share your methods or ideas in order to be part of your connection.

When looking for a connection it is not essential that you find *someone who shares your denomination.* I have been in a room with 800 other pastors in my denomination and have felt very alone. Not because they were inhospitable or disinterested in my particular ministry. Ministry connections simply cannot be legislated.

The 1996 General Conference of The United Methodist Church established The Order of Elders, which instructed all the ordained elders in each annual conference to establish relationships with each other for support, prayer, encouragement and accountability. After four years of trying to enact such legislation, it could be called a mass failure. Very few groups remained together and those that did were connected to each other *before* it was legislated. It is not essential that you find someone in your denomination to connect with. In fact, in your community, you may have a closer connection to an individual or a community of faith that lies outside your denomination.

At The Orchard, we share ministry with more congregations that are not United Methodist than congregations that are. We simply have more in common with many of them than our own sister churches within the denomination. We should not be surprised when this is so on a personal level among pastors as well. Which leads to another truth about these connections;

When looking for a connection it is not essential that you find *someone who shares your theology.* The kinds of supportive relationships that we must seek in ministry aren't anchored in theology anyway. They are anchored in our humanity and in our shared call. Over the past several years, one of my closest kindred relationships was with the pastor of an evangelical free church who theologically was a staunch Calvinist. I, on the other hand, am as staunchly Wesleyan. However, I don't ever recall us discussing theology; most times we talked about ministry and about what God was doing regardless of how we interpreted what God was doing. It is not essential that your connection be based on a shared theology.

Essential Connections

So what does an essential connection look like and where do you find one? An essential connection is *someone who shares your heart.* John Wesley once said, "If your heart is as my heart, give me your hand." What is most essential in finding someone to journey with is someone whose heart is as your heart. That means finding someone who *shares your priorities.* If your priority is creativity, or souls, or justice, or risk-taking, or fun, or laughter—whatever it is, find someone with whom you share ministry and life priorities. The four guys that are in my connection all have families that we adore. We covenant together not to lose our families just because we are in ministry. We enjoy laughing together and eating together and we do a lot of both every time we are together. If someone wants to study a lot or share deep spiritual truths, they will likely want to find a group other than ours, because, though we value those two things deeply, they are not the priority for our time together.

Your Own Annual Conference

One of the most frustrating meetings I had ever attended had just concluded and I walked out with one of our Bishops. I shared my frustration with him and asked him how he survived. As one of a very few progressive Bishops in my denomination, I suggested that he must get horribly frustrated. He said, he indeed did get very frustrated at times, but his life-line was that he and a few other bishops held their own annual conference — their own little "you are not crazy" gatherings. He also suggested to me that while I had denominationally required meetings and that my participation was important, he stressed to me not to seek my encouragement there. Instead, he instructed me to have my own annual conference.

When annual conferences were first established in United Methodism they existed for the training, encouraging and preparation of the pastors who gathered annually to share stories of what God was doing in their work and to pray for one another. Now annual conference gatherings are primarily for reporting and for action and have taken on more of the tone of a legislative branch of government than bearing the marks of those early gatherings.

What the Bishop was encouraging me to do was, in addition to attending the required gathering, to gather some friends who with me would return to the original intent of annual conferencing and hold our own meeting. Thus, now I attend two annual conferences — one out of duty and the other out of joy!

Sometimes You Are Crazy

Anyone in ministry knows there are times when what seems like a good idea in reality isn't. Everyone has been guilty of opening their mouth when they should have kept it closed or of taking a risk that transgresses the boundaries of good sense. There are times when as much as we wish someone would tell us, "you are not crazy" that we are honest with ourselves we know that we are. Even the very best of us need people who tell us when we *are* crazy. If you develop a connection that encourages and strengthens you in ministry and life, a connection that is safe and loving those same people who have repeatedly encouraged us to go to the edge, will lovingly call us back.

Conclusion

Ministry will beat the hell out of you. The non-essential connections won't do anything to restore you. They are not, in and of themselves bad connections. But when we sacrifice essential connections because of obligations to non-essential ones we jeopardize our spiritual, emotional, physical and mental health.

Find an essential connection. Someone to take the journey with then get together with them regularly and say those life-giving words to one another—"You are not crazy"—hear them for yourself and praise God for those kinds of friends.

CHAPTER 11

Trend or Event?

*O*n one of the first weekends, that we were having preview/practice services leading up to our launch day, I went away on a spiritual retreat (Emmaus Walk) and let a retired minister we had in our group preach for me. When I returned home Wendy met me at the door hugged my neck, gave me a kiss and then began crying uncontrollably. I, afraid something was seriously wrong, quickly entered listening mode and asked what had happened that upset her so. She went into a litany of things that hadn't gone right during that morning's service and then expressed her fear at how very fragile our church plant was and that no one would show up for worship if what had happened that morning happened again!

I expressed appropriate concern (one of my finer moments as a listening husband), but then told her something that had to come straight from the Holy Spirit because I had never before considered it, but it became our sanity check throughout the rest of the church planting adventure. God spoke to me and I spoke these words to her: "Never treat an event like a trend."

From that moment, every time we considered some event or action that hadn't turned out exactly like we imagined we would ask ourselves if what happened was an event—something that happened once and was unlikely to happen again—or if it was a trend—something that was a symptom of a noticeable recurring pattern. This question kept us from taking a failure too seriously, but it also kept us from lying to ourselves about successes. We had to ask, in instances where something exceeded our expectations, "Was this an anomaly or can we expect this again?"

One of the truths that we have discovered as vital to the emotional health of pastors and churches alike is an honest appraisal of how they are doing. One way to be honest with yourself is to *Never treat an event like a trend* and *Never treat a trend like an event.* In other words, don't get too high or too low when evaluating an event—don't overestimate its impact. In addition, at the same time don't kid yourself into thinking that a significant trend is too localized—don't underestimate its impact. The only way I know to apply this rule is to evaluate constantly.

Evaluate Constantly

It has been said, "What counts gets measured and what gets measured counts." I would add to that one further sentence: "If it doesn't count, don't measure it." (maybe even: if it doesn't count, don't do it!)

Churches that are growing and healthy are constantly taking inventory of their health and the areas where improvement it needed. The only way to not look at a trend like an event or your events as trends is to know your trends. Asking the two questions which serve as the centerpiece for this chapter must be part of a larger evaluation process which looks each ministry and events in the congregation and determines their fruitfulness (John 15:16) or potential for bearing fruit.

Evaluate Worship

At The Orchard every Monday morning at 8: with a team of people who have the primary r for carrying out the Sunday Morning Worship in hand we take a look at every aspect of the service: music, transitions, worship, video, offering and any other pieces of the service—especially the sermon.

If worship and/or sermons are to improve, those leading have to make an honest (or should I say ruthless) evaluation of them regularly. Sometimes we listen or watch services together. I regularly watch the sermon video in order to distinguish habitual speech patterns, phrases or physical gestures. I want great sermons to be a trend at The Orchard, but if they are going to be then it means that I have to be constantly listening to and improving my study and communications skills.

The other components of the worship service must be carefully scrutinized too. Was the song singable? Were the transitions smooth? Did the video, if one was used, communicate clearly? Did anything happen on stage that was a subtraction rather than an addition to the service? The reason you ask these questions about each part of the service is because if week in week out a particular place, piece or person in the service subtracts from the service—then you can decide it is a trend—even though it is a negative one and act to correct the mistake.

Evaluate Ministries

The same evaluation that you use to look at worship must also be used to look at every other aspect of the ministry of your church. The standard or rule that you measure by is the stated mission and vision of your church.

Each year, before budget time the staff considers each ministry of the past year and asks: "Did this ministry bear fruit for Christ's Kingdom?" "Did the ministry help someone grow deep in the love of Jesus or branch out to someone with he love of Jesus?" The ministries that pass this accounting get funding in the upcoming budget. Those that do not pass this test don't receive funding. The exception to this rule is if we recognize that a particular ministry may take longer than one budget year to significantly begin to yield fruit.

These questions that we use to evaluate ministries reflect the vision of The Orchard: Devoted to the cultivation of fruit for Christ's Kingdom. They also reflect the mission: helping people grow deep in the love of Jesus and branch out to others with that love.

Without constant evaluation valuable resources of money, time and energy are misdirected to ministries that have little or no potential for fruitfulness. Over a relatively short period of time the result are ministries whose trend is lack of fruit for Christ's Kingdom, irrespective of the resources invested in them.

Evaluate Events

Every year every church I know holds annual events for no other purpose than "we have always held that event." Homecomings, Vacation Bible Schools, Revivals, and Singing Schools are just a number of events that keep getting repeated in congregations all across the land with no real measure of effectiveness ever being considered. My own denomination is overflowing with "we have always held that event" events. Each year in Mississippi Methodism we have twenty-eight different Sunday service emphases we are supposed to celebrate! Many of them are for long outdated programs, but we have always celebrated those ministries so we just keep on keeping on.

A healthy church evaluates each event they hold not only for excellence, but also for effectiveness regarding their overall mission and vision.

At The Orchard, following a major event like Vacation Bible School (which we call InsideOut) or our Fall Festival

Outreach the whole staff gives feedback to the staff person who was in charge of the event. What went well? What didn't? Did we accomplish the purpose set out for the event? If we had to do the event again next year, what would we change? If we didn't have to do the event again next year, would we do it again?

This constant evaluation keeps us from spending enormous amounts of time, energy, and resources on something that does not accomplish our purposes or move us along toward the fulfillment of our mission and vision.

We evaluate our Easter and Christmas services the very same way. Not that we wouldn't do Easter or Christmas! But, so much special emphasis goes on these two seasons that we evaluate our marketing, outreaches, events, worship services, and ultimately the results. Jesus appointed us to go and bear fruit—fruit that will last (John 15.16). I expect that he would expect that we spend our efforts doing what will bear the most fruit. That means evaluating our "garden plots." And it also means evaluating our gardeners.

Evaluate Staff

Healthy churches evaluate their staff. Every year in November every staff member is evaluated. This evaluation serves as an opportunity to celebrate their victories, to discover what they have learned from their mistakes, and to chart a course of continued fruitfulness for the coming year.

At The Orchard, staff members complete an evaluation instrument that includes their evaluation of the Senior Pastor (a copy of this instrument is available by email request to becominganorchard@theorchard.net). Every staff member uses the instrument to evaluate their work during the past year and to announce goals for the upcoming year. I complete the same form on each staff person. Then we sit down together to look at both evaluations and draw some conclusions that affect their salary and their future employment. The end result is an agreed upon letter grade for their work.

Assigning a letter grade is a concrete way of communicating the quality of the work of any staff person. Everyone understands what an A+ is. Likewise, everyone understands what a D is! A-level performers are rewarded considerably; B-level performers are rewarded modestly; C-level performers are not rewarded at all; and D-level performers are looking for a job! After the letter grades have been assigned and each staff member and I have come to a mutual agreement regarding their evaluation, The Orchard's Personnel Team reviews the evaluations for consistency and fairness. The Personnel Team also checks that actions plans, remediation or further discussions take place if need be.

There are numerous reasons that the Church has been ineffective in accomplishing its mission. I believe one significant reason is that we have not held its leaders accountable for effective leading and continued professional and personal growth. Healthy churches regularly evaluate their staff in order to identify people who can lead the church toward healthy and fruitful trends and away from unproductive practices and ministries.

Conclusion

Never treat a trend like an event; nor an event like a trend. Keep a clear perspective on the effectiveness of your church. One clear way to do this is to evaluate everything you do. It takes time to evaluate every ministry and event. However, the time that it takes to use this valuable tool will save us a great deal of time wasted on ministries and events that do not accomplish Jesus' directive to his disciples—"Go and bear fruit."—which is clearly the trend that Jesus expected.

CHAPTER 12

Denomination as a *Starting* Place

⊹━━⊹

In August of 2001, I was near Quito, Ecuador on a short-term mission trip with a group from The Orchard. We were staying in the dormitories at SEMISUD, which is the largest South American Seminary for The Church of God of Cleveland denomination. On the way to my room, I met one of the General Secretaries of The United Methodist Church. He was there as part of a World Council of Churches delegation who had come to South America to dialogue with Pentecostal churches about their unwillingness to participate with the WCC. He was amazed to find a United Methodist Congregation doing what they had traveled thousands of miles to discuss. Amazed, he asked me about how we, a United Methodist Church, were able to work out a partnership with the Church of God of Cleveland Seminary. My reply was simply, "because we are both more interested in the kingdom than in the denomination."

One of the principles of growth that stands out about vibrant congregations is that the denomination is a starting place, but it is not their final destination.

Mission of the Annual Conference

The stated mission of the Mississippi Annual Conference of The United Methodist Church is to equip the church to make disciples for Jesus Christ. That is an outstanding mission, fully on target, one that is true to our call. However, theory and practice can prove to be radically different, even in well-intentioned denominations.

Denominations, if not kept in their proper perspective, can demand so much of the pastor's time and the church's attention that they actually prevent us from accomplishing its and our stated mission—to make disciples of Jesus Christ.

If the denomination you serve in is multi-layered—existing at local, districts, conferences (state level) and general church levels there are as many as three levels *outside* your local congregation which may require quarterly or more frequent meetings. This does not even account for the preparation, subcommittee or telephone work that must be done in between meetings.

At one point early in my ministry, through my own lack of discipline, I served on three denominational committees and served as chair on one of them. This meant a combined total of nine annual meetings, plus preparation meetings with subcommittees and any informal discussions necessary to understand the task at hand! All this while leading a fledgling, but rapidly growing congregation made me put off high priority tasks in order to accomplish urgent tasks. Something had to give.

Denominations aren't evil, or insidious or intentionally distracting. The Orchard is part of a denomination that holds great promise and provides many benefits to its member churches (we will discuss this later in the chapter). However, denominations are not the most efficient organizations and the maintenance of them can often drain a church or its staff of the emotional, spiritual and time resources unless the proper perspective is maintained. What is that proper perspective, in my opinion?

The Local Church is the primary place of ministry

When deciding how I will spend my time, and mental, emotional, and spiritual resources, the local church and its ministries always top my priority list. At the local church level, I meet, lead and minister to the particular people God has sent me to. If I don't initiate ministry at the local church level, who will?

One of my passions is planting churches. In 1998, I was returning from a year of intensive training for church planting. While planting The Orchard, I was also serving on the Denomination's New Church Development Committee for the state of Mississippi. I poured an enormous amount of time and energy into helping revise our state plan for identifying, training and deploying pastors who could plant churches. Along with a team of other pastors, we also changed the church plant funding process so that our plants had more latitude in getting started. All the planning, while very tiring, was exciting. The opportunity to make drastic changes to an ineffective church planting methodology was worth the price. When we presented the plan to the statewide assembly (the annual conference) we met shocking resistance. What made the resistance most difficult to accept was that the opposition to the change was using misinformation to oppose the plan. Never, have I been more disappointed at a denominational level.

Out of that experience, I concluded that the best way to affect change at the denominational level was to show the way at the local church level. Augustine's words may be particularly helpful here: Preach the Gospel everywhere and if necessary use words!" The denomination may be able to argue with your argument, but they can't argue with an obviously effective approach to ministry.

The local church must be the primary location of ministry and transformation of the denomination must take place by the overflow of the local church. This is not only the most effective way of transformation; it is also the most congruent with the call of the Gospel. We are called first and foremost to be builders of Christ's Kingdom, not our denominations.

Builders of Christ's Kingdom

In John chapter fifteen, verse sixteen, Jesus makes very clear the mission of the disciples. They were to go and bear fruit that would last. No one would argue that Jesus meant that the disciples would add people to the Kingdom (see John 4). Somewhere along the way Jesus disciples began grouping and in grouping became more concerned with adding to their group than in fulfilling Jesus' mandate.

In any community there is plenty of Kingdom work to be done. Jesus himself recognized that the fields were ripe for harvest, but the laborers were few (John 4:36). Statistically in any community of 50 to 5 million, 50 percent (or more) of the residents do not have a personal relationship with Jesus or a connection to a community of faith. Some would argue that this is simply not so in their community. My response is that they simply do not hang around the right kind of wrong people.

This statistic should inform our work in several ways. First, if 50% of the people in our community do not have a personal relationship with Jesus or a connection to a community of faith I am not in competition with the other churches in town because there are plenty of people to go around. The real competition is every other available use of a person's time. We are not competing with other churches in our community. We are competing against soccer, t-ball, sitcoms, bunko groups and the like. Any time people choose to be in a growing discipleship process it is a Kingdom win.

Secondly, we need to be supportive of the other churches in our community because we are not trying to make the next generation of Methodists (or Baptists, etc.). We are trying to make the next generation of Christians. This is not an idea that is popular with denominations. But pastors or denominational leaders who lament a family who joins the next church down the road instead of ours have a very narrow view of the Kingdom of Christ. In Tupelo, there are 20,000 unchurched people. If one person joins the local Presbyterian Church, then that only leaves 19,999 to go. That is a Kingdom win.

The reason we so often miss this is that we are focused on who we do have—how many people attend our church in comparison to the other churches in town or in our denomination. We must stay focused on our target group, the group to whom we were sent—those in our community who are outside the Kingdom.

Third, we need to partner with the other churches in our community because if all the unchurched people in our community decided to show up at our church this Sunday, our church wouldn't hold them all. The only hope we have of reaching the whole community is if the whole Body of Christ is focused on this task. Competitiveness among churches and between denominations is counterproductive to the Kingdom. It only confirms to those who are outside the Kingdom what they suspected all along—that we are petty.

Finally, we need to help people find a place to belong, even if they belong at another church. This is true because we are in the business of helping people find and enter into a relationship with God. If they can do that better somewhere else, we should encourage them to do so. It should be no big deal if a family or 10 families leave our church as long as they attend another one. If we are focused on the outsiders there are plenty of people there to replace them.

For these reasons one of the primary principles of growth in healthy churches is that they will partner with anyone who is Kingdom focused. Jesus shows us the way in this matter in Mark 9:

> "Teacher," said John, "we saw a man driving out demons in your name and we told him to stop, because he was not one of us. "Do not stop him," Jesus said. "No one who does a miracle in my name can in the next moment say anything bad about me, for whoever is not against us is for us. I tell you the truth, anyone who gives you a cup of water in my name because you belong to Christ will certainly not lose his reward.

Partners with anyone who Kingdom Focused

The Orchard will partner with anyone who is Kingdom focused. We will tell you everything we know and about all the mistakes we have made along the way. Maybe you can do it better than we can and then we can in turn learn from you. This means that though we are obligated by denominational bonds to help our denominational churches that we are not prohibited from helping any and every church by sharing what God has taught us and in some cases the resources God has blessed us with.

Between 2002 and 2004, we helped plant five new churches. One was Presbyterian and the other two were Independent. We also helped plant two new Methodist Churches. Our involvement included coaching, sharing of resources and financial underwriting of all five of these congregations. We recognize the need for unique Kingdom focused ministries in our communities and have strived to partner with them to reach the unchurched in our community and we expect that our involvement will not only continue but also expand!

Church planting is not our only area of partnering. We share a food pantry and clothes closet with two other churches and have worked on Habitat for Humanity Projects with many other denominations.

In our community we are also actively seeking a formal partnership with an African-American Congregation as a means of growing together in faith and in reaching out to our community. It appears that this formal partnership with lie outside our denominational church in Tupelo.

Body of Christ

This is what it means to be the Body of Christ. Just as within any community of faith (church) there are many and diverse gifts, within the church universal there are particular roles that each denomination plays. There are appealing (and not so appealing) aspects to each of these groups. But we need each other. For the reasons recounted in this chapter and for hundreds more that have not even been considered—we need each other if we are ever going to reach our communities. This will become more and more apparent to us when we are honest enough to admit to ourselves that by ourselves we will never reach everyone in our community—as bad as we hate to admit it—not everyone will like us or be attracted to Jesus at our church. But if we remember that our primary task is building the Kingdom then we can work together to do so.

Denominational Benefits

It has been my suggestion in this chapter that in healthy churches, denominational distinction must be a starting place and not an ending place. I believe this so strongly because I see so many of my own denominational churches turned inward and avoiding partnerships that truly would expand the Kingdom of Christ in their community. Likewise, I felt the cold avoidance of other denominational churches that would not associate with our church because we were not of their theological persuasion.

This is not to say that denominations and affiliations do not have their benefits. I have a friend who left the United Methodist Church and began an Independent Church. For the whole life of the congregation they have been in a doctrinal argument about even the simplest matters of faith. Denominations have core tenets of doctrine and belief that their churches can point to as foundational understandings to be upheld.

When starting a new work this is particularly helpful because you attract people with no idea of what to believe and they soon form their own opinions. Many of them also believe their opinion is the right one! However, if you are beginning a denominational church you have hundreds of years of thought, discernment and wisdom to point to as your guide and rule in the matter.

Denominations also provide for natural collegial relationships, and for accountability, support and guidance in administrative and spiritual matters.

My intent in this chapter has not been to tear down denominations. It has been to recognize that the problem is not the denomination, but the people who lose perspective on them. Denominations must be a starting place, not an ending one.

Conclusion

Denominations can be great partners in ministry. Nevertheless, they can also be great distractions. Perspective is needed — and the perspective I advocate is that Denominations are instruments for building Christ's Kingdom. They go awry when they begin to pour resources into building their own kingdom or distract their pastors from the primary task — bearing fruit for Christ's Kingdom (John 15.16).

CHAPTER 13

Holy Patience with the Unholy

He hung around after the service to ask me an important question. Jack wanted to know if he would be "welcomed here." I answered that I hoped he already had been since we were through with the service. But he pressed on to tell me about how he was a misfit. He fit the part: disheveled, clothes worn thin, thinning hair, in need of a bath and walking with a severe limp, feeling as much a relational misfit because by his own admission Jack was homosexual. He was moving from a town, to our town because there was no place for his "kind" in their town, and he began looking for a church where he could attend because he had promised his daughter he would attend church if they would just relocate.

What was as unusual as Jack's story was the way he found The Orchard. After arriving in town, he and his daughter went to the local library and began to search online for a church where they would be welcomed given their "misfit" status. After hours looking online Jack didn't feel like there were any churches in Tupelo that looked promising, so, after telling his story to the librarian at the reference desk he quizzed her if she knew a church where they would be welcomed. Her response is one of the most prized compliments The Orchard has ever received. She said, "You need to go the The Orchard. They take anybody." What made this statement even more complimentary is that the reference librarian attended a different church!

At The Orchard, we understand that it takes an incredible amount of patience with people who are coming to faith. While we will never tell people that a lifestyle of life-taking habits are acceptable, but we will walk with them in patience as God coaxes them toward his life-giving way.

The Visit

Several times a year, a new visitor or family to The Orchard will make an appointment to talk to me about membership. By now, after several of these appointments, I am well prepared for the conversation that is about to happen.

Generally, the couple will come in, sit down and begin with compliments about our church. "We really love the music." Or "We really enjoy the sermon" or some other encouragement. Eventually they get around to saying, "We really love The Orchard; we just can't join. See, we live next door to some people who say this is their church home. In fact, they invited us. But do you know what they do during the week? If that is the kind of church this is then we can't join."

My response usually shocks them. "I do know what they are doing during the week. I know it seems inconsistent for someone who goes to church and calls The Orchard their church home. But you should have seen them last year!"

My point is that we cannot expect people who are not Christians to act like Christians until they are. Furthermore, we cannot expect new Christians to act like mature Christians when they aren't. Some of them have had absolutely no faith models. They don't know they shouldn't act a certain way, go certain places, or do certain things until someone tells them and the Holy Spirit convicts them!

Problem with Christians

One of the problems Christians have in reaching people who do not have a personal relationship with Jesus is that after they have been a Christian for a while they do not know anyone who does not have a personal relationship with Jesus. They spend most of their time with Christians and eventually Christian behavior becomes the expected norm so much so that they cannot tolerate anyone who does not act like or sometimes even think like a Christian.

Recently, one of the professionals that attends The Orchard invited me to share lunch with him and a colleague who was not interested in attending church. The friend objected that he could not reasonably accept that God saved every species on earth from a worldwide flood by having a man named Noah build a big boat. That was his objection to church—that some of the stories seemed unreasonable. So I simply told him to believe what he wanted to believe about Noah and the Ark. Furthermore, I told him it was of no consequence to me if he believed that story or not, because the belief of central importance was that God wanted to have a relationship with him so badly that he was willing to die to establish even the possibility of that relationship.

In that lunch hour he became open to the possibility of a relationship because I was the first one to tell him that it was o.k. to question (and even not believe at this point) the story of Noah and the Ark. He had been in arguments (his word) with Christian friends about this very matter. However, they always ended up pushing the "you just have to have faith" button to end the argument. A bright, intelligent, reasoning young man wouldn't consider faith because of the behavior of Christians. Isn't this exactly the opposite of what we hope for?

Problem with Churches

The problem is no less prominent in churches. Too often our churches expect that people who come to church will behave themselves both inside and outside the church. The church needs to be reminded that we cannot expect people to act like Christians until they are and then only as the church takes the responsibility to teach them everything Jesus commanded (Matthew 28:20).

Now as in Jesus day it is easy to understand why Jesus had to emphasize that he came for the sick, because the religious leaders forget that truth in light of their preference for the whitewashed. Therefore, those who do attend church feel the need to pretend and those who cannot pretend simply do not attend! At The Orchard we deal with severely broken people every day. I don't think that we have proportionately more broken people; I just believe we create a climate where more people feel they can tell the truth about their lives. Churches must say loudly and clearly, "you don't have to have it all together to attend here." Then they have to communicate Christ's hope that with God's guidance, we will figure it out together.

This means that a pastor may spend more time reading the felony arrests than the obituaries. They may spend late nights picking up parishioners from bars or visiting them in jail. However, the pastor who communicates this through relationship and through the constant affirmation that "there is a place for you here" will find that they have a ministry in the nature and character of Christ.

It is very tiring work, because just when you think there are no new ways for people to self-destruct they will invent three new ways. Sometimes you will want to throw up your hands and quit. However, most of the time, when the moment of grace comes, when you can see them with Jesus' eyes, then your heart and your patience for this ministry grows.

This became crystal clear to me on a visit to a men's prison. The chaplain who had invited our church there to lead a Thanksgiving service was giving us a tour of one of the units before the service began. As we walked down the aisles between the beds of the brightly lit unit, men were talking, bathing, reading and sleeping. As we neared the end of one of the aisles there was a man sleeping. Curled up like a little boy, this grown man reminded me of the three-year old I had left at home that night. Someone had given birth, nurtured, and loved this child. At one time he too had been three and was busy running, jumping, throwing and breaking things. I had an overwhelming realization that this was someone's child. And in that moment God whispered in my spirit—"yes Bryan, he's *my* child."

Try looking at the people in your world through Jesus' eyes. Our churches are full of older brothers, but we must keep our eyes fixed on the horizon for the return of the prodigals. Only a home where they believe they will be welcomed will stir in them the idea that they can return home.

Salvation is a Process

Those who would object to extended patience need look no further than John Wesley's order of salvation. In which he noted there was prevenient grace (the grace that goes before); justifying grace (which makes us right with God) and sanctifying grace (which works in us to make us like Christ). It is clearly a work and not an instantaneous transformation that makes us act, think and love like Jesus. So while we are saved in an instant, we are also in the process of being saved. When prodigals know that home is the best place for the process to be fostered in their lives *and* they know that those at home will be patient with them, even help them figure out the way forward they are more likely to climb out of the pigpen (Luke 15)

Great Patience

Want to know what it takes reach prodigals? A message of hope (which we have) and great patience as that hope seeps into the lives of those who feel hopeless.

In the summer of 1999, I began to run a low-grade fever. It persisted for almost three months and was accompanied by lethargy, night sweats and cold chills. During the first couple of days I assumed it was simply a virus that would run its course so I didn't run to the doctor. After a week of worsening, however, I was miserable and beginning to worry that something more significant than a virus was affecting me. I am not usually one who runs to the doctor, but by day seven I was so miserable I wanted to see the doctor. What if I had said to myself, "I am miserable; I don't know what is wrong with me; I don't know if the doctor can help me, but he says he can. However, the doctor has declared that he doesn't want me in his office. In fact to go see the doctor I have to be well. He doesn't want someone with a problem in his office because it will make him look bad, like he doesn't know what he is doing. So until I can figure out for myself what is wrong and fix it, I won't go to the doctor."

No one thinks that way—about doctors. But they think that way all the time about churches. There are broken, hurting, sin-sick people who think they have to be well before they can come to our office. Do you want to know where they got that idea? From us (the Church)!

Over the course of the next two and a half months I saw numerous doctors had several tests and discovered I had walking pneumonia. I could have never figured that one out by myself. Nor could I have treated myself. People who were patient and knowledgeable and interested came alongside me to restore me.

They referred to me as their *patient*. Remembering what we once were, may help us to be patient...so that all may be welcomed into their Father's house.

CHAPTER 14

Development
not just Deployment

+══════+

*O*ccasionally I am asked to speak to groups about what
is happening at The Orchard and why I believe what
is happening is happening. People are usually interested, but
at some point in the dialogue, they begin to get a glazed look
on their eyes. At first, I thought, "Oh no, I am boring them
out of their minds!" But I have come to discover (at least I
hope I am being honest with myself) that they are not bored
they are just speculative. At some point in my litany about
The Orchard they begin to wonder if what we do can be done
where they serve and in some way begin to mentally assess
if *I* could do what I do where they serve.

The first couple of times I noticed the glazed look, I
ignored it and continued with my presentation. However, the
glazed look became more and more prevalent and appeared
earlier in the presentation so I had to choose to lose the group
or address the question they were all thinking. This realization came to me one day when one of the workshop partici-
pants asked very directly, "I want to know what you would

do if they appointed you to a 150 year old traditional church tomorrow?" My answer that day was (and continues to be to this day): I would build the church I want around the church I have. I am not the originator of this idea. My mentor, Dr. Dale Galloway, the now retired Founding Pastor of New Hope Community Church in Portland, Oregon taught this principle repeatedly during a year I spent with him in the Beeson Pastor Program at Asbury Theological Seminary. But the more I have considered his assertion, the more I am convinced that "building the church I want around the church I have" is exactly the approach I would take.

Pastors are practical animals, though, and what I thought was a sufficient answer to the workshop participant was only partially satisfying. He pressed me even further asking, "And where would you begin that building?" This time, much more certain of my answer, I offered, "I would start with leadership development."

Why Begin There?

Well the easy answer is that you have to begin somewhere! The more specific answer is there is nowhere else you will see more rapid change than if you invest in leaders who help you spread the message. Leadership development is exponential time.

You can spend your time trying to navigate ministries or programs through your congregation's approval system or you can shape leaders who will do it for you. You can spend time making all the decisions so that you keep the congregation on track toward the desired destination or you can shape leaders who will not only help you make those decisions but eventually make those decisions without you. You can spend time at a different committee meeting every night of the week making sure that all the outcomes contribute to the overall ministry health of the congregation or you can shape leaders who can meet, decide and execute those outcomes without you directing every step.

Leadership Development time is exponential time because you are shaping an army of people who see what you see, desire what you desire, and act accordingly. Now this does not mean they will always choose your means to the end, but as long as they choose the right end the congregation wins! This does not happen quickly, or easily, but when it happens it is incredibly rewarding for you as a leader and it is incredibly beneficial to the congregation as a whole.

This intentional approach begins with understanding the difference between development and deployment.

Development not just Deployment

Many congregations have people who are leading ministries or emphases of the church but not really leading the church as a whole. Interestingly enough, we often separate people out to make decisions for the whole, who don't get the whole picture either. That is because, generally, the church is good at delegation or deployment but not at development.

Delegation means that you do what we tell you to do on our behalf. We decide, and then you act. In some cases, it even means I, the pastor, decide and you act. Either way, no one acts without someone telling them what to do. In general, a church's list of officers is full of people who have been delegated responsibility in areas of evangelism, youth, worship, buildings and grounds, or any number of other task areas. In essence, people have been identified and deployed to take care of the church's interests, and in most cases, these are people, whose only training for doing so is that they have an expressed interest in that area.

If we are honest with ourselves, we also recognize that there are people leading some of those areas because we have persuaded them to do so—not because they have an interest or training or a passion, but because we have a need. The church has hundreds of years of proven skill at delegation and deployment and very little experience with development of leaders.

The one exception to this rule (and even that can be argued) is the development of a professional clergy. Seminaries and Judicatories train and deploy professional ministers. Noticeably absent from their training, however, are the skills necessary to develop others as leaders in the local congregation. Seminaries train, and Judicatories expect that pastors are there to do the work of the congregation, thus congregations often adopt just such an attitude. However, the Body of Christ includes the priesthood of all believers and should evidence a well-trained, developed lay leadership group. The primary responsibility for this development should rest squarely on the shoulders of the primary leader—the pastor.

The Benefits

Aside from the benefits alluded to earlier in this chapter, there are countless other reasons that leadership development is essential in the vibrant community of faith.

The first good reason is that Leadership Development is Scriptural. Paul wrote to Timothy: You then, my son, be strong in the grace that is in Christ Jesus. And the things you have heard me say in the presence of many witnesses entrust to reliable men who will also be qualified to teach others (2 Timothy 2:2). Think of what the Asian churches would have been like if Paul had tried to teach at all of them all of the time. Of course, this would have been physically impossible during Paul's time, but Paul didn't even attempt to micromanage them. He taught them until he was convinced that leaders were in place to continue the Kingdom progress of the congregation, and then he moved on. It didn't mean that he never had to provide some corrective developmental instruction—that is precisely what each of his letters are—he reminds them, instructs them, and shapes them for continued Kingdom impact and faithfulness.

None of us have the number of churches that Paul had to care for. However, many of us have a number of ministries that we must give direction and oversight to. We have much to learn from Paul's supervision of New Testament Churches as we develop leaders who can lead those ministries in ways that impact the Kingdom of Christ that is consistent with the overall health of the congregation.

Another notable benefit of leadership development is that you train people to problem-solve without you. When you develop this kind of leadership culture solutions you never dreamed of emerge. I remember the first time I knew that our leadership development approach was blossoming. There had been plenty of little decisions and little victories along the way. But one Sunday night at our monthly leadership team meeting there was a staff issue that needed to be settled, and both the Leadership Team Chairman and I knew that it would involve significant discussion—and I believed significant input from me. During the meeting the staff issue was raised, discussion ensued, a conclusion was drawn, and an implementation plan was enacted, and I never had a chance to enter into the discussion. In that moment, God spoke into my spirit, "Bryan, enjoy this. It is what you have been waiting for." And I did.

This kind of decision-making can only happen with developed leaders. It can never happen with leaders who are simply deployed because they take their cues from the leader/ pastor. This culture has been so developed in our congregation, that I was on vacation when the Leadership Team met to discuss the $200,000 worth of potential overages on our $6 million building project. The Leadership Team Chair assured me that they didn't need me to change my plans! The reason he could say this and I could accept it with complete confidence is that he and I spend time together every week. He understands as clearly as I do our vision, mission, and core values. He understands our stewardship commitments and the way The Orchard feels about the resources entrusted to our care. I knew that we were committed to the same thing—the right thing—not simply his idea or my idea.

Additionally, leaders who develop leaders are freer to devote themselves to listening to God's call for the future because they have developed leaders to lead the present. This is not to say that your leaders shouldn't be involved in listening for the future. But clearly it is the pastor who has the larger amount of time that can be devoted to such a task.

Finally, the greatest reward of leadership development is that you become expendable. You actually can go home on a night the finance team meets. You can go on vacation without your cell phone ringing every hour. You can mentally lay down the burdens of decision making from time to time because you know you are not the only one whose aim is to do what is best for the congregation. The quality of your leadership development work will be judged only after you are gone. Will the church flourish or falter after you are gone? In the mean time, however, you can get a fair evaluation of your process by considering how indispensable you are now.

In reality, a culture of leadership development instead of deployment affords the pastor *and* the congregation countless benefits as they seek to advance the Kingdom. How is this culture shaped?

Leadership Team

It begins with the careful selection of the people who will lead your congregation. Some would interject that you don't always have control over who leads your congregation. You inherit some leaders, and there are some significant influencers who don't hold formal leadership positions in your church. However, if you carefully choose those who will serve in formal leadership roles and spend time with those you inherit, I believe you can shape both groups toward a consistent destination—one that expands the Kingdom and is good for the overall health of the local congregation.

One of the finest leaders I know is The Orchard's seventy-five year old treasurer, Karl Cornwell. Karl and his wife Gerri were part of our original core group. Karl was an entrepreneur and had served as the nationwide controller for Montgomery Ward stores in earlier years and he became the treasurer during the startup phase of The Orchard. When Karl and Gerri showed up at that first core group gathering and I cast the vision for The Orchard, I was sure they wouldn't come back. In their late sixties at that time, I figured this new creative expression of church would not appeal to them. I supposed that they were set in their understanding of church and wouldn't be interested in changing their expectations. What I found, however, was a questioning mind and a sincere heart for what The Orchard was trying to do. Karl would come by the office every week and we would sit down for two hours to drink coffee and pay the bills. If I had only been interested in paying the bills, we could have finished the task in half an hour. But, I was as interested in shaping one of the primary influencers in our congregation. Today, Karl is one of my most trusted advisers, and I can think of no one I respect more than him. Part of that respect is because of his impeccable character and part of that respect is because, even at his age, he was willing to endure a young energetic pastor's dreams, and dare to dream along with him. That dreaming was made possible by a little extra time paying the bills.

On another note, you should only select leaders who have the capacity to see the congregation's whole picture perspective. If you only have five you only choose five. Don't feel obligated to have a minimum size board until you have at least that number of available leaders who see the whole picture. If no one in your congregations is a whole picture person, then choose three people and begin developing them by spending an enormous amount of time with them.

One extremely important aspect of leader selection is to not assign them (or choose them) as representatives of a particular area of the church. For example, don't have a youth representative, a children's ministry representative and an older adult representative. When people are assigned to represent a certain area of ministry it encourages them to be territorial. In addition, when we feel we have to choose people to represent a particular ministry area on our Leadership Team, we can feel pressured to pick someone that may not have the capacity to see the whole ministry picture. By making everyone on your leadership team responsible for every area, it forces them to look at how each decision affects the whole and not just their one particular area.

When training these individuals make sure they know who they work for. Each year, when we gather our leaders in January for Orientation, I make my "Know who you work for" speech. It goes something like this: This is not a democracy, and you are not elected officials. You do not have to run for re-election, so don't feel like you have to please your constituents — whomever that may be in the church. You are set apart specifically to answer one question in all matters. That one question is not, "what does my small group want?' or "what do parents want?" or "what does the music ministry want?" Neither is that one question, "what do I want?" or "what does Bryan want?" The one question that we must strive repeatedly to answer and for which we will be held accountable is this: In this matter "What does God want?" This is not a democracy. We will not win or lose based on votes. This is a theocracy — we want to do what God wants us to do. Therefore, we will wrestle together until we come to that conclusion on each and every matter.

When our leaders hear me give that speech, they do not sense that they should not listen to their constituents, or that they should not enter into dialogue with one another in decision-making. However, we all are clear about what our objective is and that helps keep us from misdirected decisions.

I cannot begin to explain the spiritual high you feel when you see your leaders lay aside their personal preferences to choose what is best for the congregation as a whole. When they decide to do what is best instead of what is easiest, you will begin to enjoy the firstfruits of developing leaders.

Give these leaders all access to you. Whatever you are doing, drop it to talk to them. Make them your priority and they will prioritize to be with you and be shaped by you. Then read books with them, have meals with them, take them to churches and conferences that are reinforcing what you are saying. It is amazing how much more credibility you gain when you are not the only one saying something. Pour your life into them and you will multiply your life and vision into people who will multiply it into others and along the way you will learn and grow with them.

This time spent with your leadership core is intense and time consuming. However, nothing has more potential to change the culture of your church than an increased number of leaders speaking and leading together.

The Leadership Crucible

There must be, however, a way to invest in other rising or potential leaders without the risk of placing them on your leadership core. One of the ways we do this at The Orchard is The Leadership Crucible.

For the past several years, one of my strongest leaders, Roger Weldon, and I spend every Tuesday morning from seven to eight a.m. teaching an interactive leadership class that we call The Leadership Crucible. A crucible is a place of forming and we want to form and identify rising and potential leaders.

The Leadership Crucible is organized in six-week terms around a particular leadership theme. Leadership is Pain; The Character of a Leader; Mentoring Other Leaders, Decision Making; Learning from Leadership Mistakes and Leadership

Priorities are just a few of the themes we have worked with over the last several years. The first week of each term we set the tone with a presentation by either Roger or me. The second week we show a video clip as a discussion piece; the third week we have a round-table discussion about the topic; on week four we have one of the group make a participant's presentation; week five usually is a "hot-seat" format in which we write questions or scenarios on note cards and have each person draw one out and lead us in working out a solution; and we wrap up the term by having a community leader address the group around the theme.

Over the years we have had some interesting discussions, but we have had extraordinary growth. The crucible has been a place to mentor next step leaders and a great place to evaluate potential leaders. It also provides leaders, including you, with an opportunity for constant growth.

Take Somebody with You

Of course the most elementary way to teach people what you want them to know is to take them with you. Hospital visits, church visits, leadership opportunities, anything you do you should do with someone who needs to see what you are seeing and have their own minds imprinted with people, places and pictures of the preferred future. Never waste the opportunity to shape leaders by performing potentially shaping tasks alone.

Self-Development

The absolutely essential aspect of developing leaders is that the primary leader (you and me) is serious about his or her own development. John Maxwell wrote about one of the most substantial leadership learnings in his book *The 21 Irrefutable Laws of Leadership*. Law #1, that Maxwell identifies is The Law of the Lid, which states that an organization and its leaders will never rise above the leadership capacity of the primary leader. He or she is the lid.

To make sure that we don't become the lid in our congregations we have to be constantly growing, learning, and stretching. There are more than enough books about personal growth (see my list of favorites at the end of the chapter) as a leader so I won't rehash "21 ways to grow as a leader" but I will share my favorite three: Reading, Conferences, and Master Minding.

Theodore Roosevelt was such a voracious reader that he read at least one book a day and if the books were small he read two or three. This was his practice while he was President of The United States. I think we can agree that he was at least as busy as most pastors are, so there really is no excuse for not reading. I believe an aggressive reading plan is absolutely necessary to aggressive growth. This reading should be as deep as it is broad. Stephen Sample in his book, *The Contrarian's Guide to Leadership* suggests that we should spend our time reading the Super Texts, which he defines as the classics and other great works, and almost no time reading the newspaper. Reading is one of the primary ways of personal leadership development.

Not much needs to be said about conferences. The United States has some of the best opportunities to grow as a leader with its numerous church and leadership conferences held annually. These conferences not only introduce you to new ideas, they remind you of old priorities and it never fails that when I am around that many learning people my mind races to places I would never have gone outside of that experience.

Finally, let me say a word about Master Minding. Master Minding is a concept a friend introduced me to pioneered by Success Coach Tommy Newberry. Master Minding is the gathering of a small diverse group of individuals for the purpose of using the collective input and thought processes to create a learning climate—a master mind that is bigger and more creative than the sum of its parts. I gather both with a group of pastors semi-annually and a group of community leaders monthly for the sole purpose of growing and learning as a leader. I do this because I don't want to be the lid.

Conclusion

Leadership development, not just leadership deployment is a shift of mind for most churches and their pastors. Many of us are so pressed for time that we don't feel like we have even one extra minute to do the hard work of leadership development. Leadership deployment and delegation is much easier, no doubt. However, we have not been called to do what is easiest, but what is best. What is best for the Kingdom, the congregation and us is the investment in others that helps them impact others for the Kingdom of Christ.

Recommended Reading:

- The Fifth Discipline by Peter Senge
- Customs and Culture by Eugene Nida
- Leadership is an Art by Max DePree
- Good to Great by Jim Collins
- Lincoln on Leadership by Donald T. Philips
- Visioneering by Andy Stanley
- The Contrarian's Guide to Leadership by Stephen Sample
- Unlearning Church by Michael Slaughter
- Courageous Leadership by Bill Hybels
- Spiritual Leadership by Oswald Sanders
- Orbiting the Giant Hairball by Gordon McKenzie
- The Leadership Challenge by James Kouzes and Barry Posner

CHAPTER 15

Outward Eyes

When Jesus reassembled with his disciples in the upper room after the resurrection he did not encourage them to stay in the upper room or to focus on themselves or to shut out the world that now, even more than before, endangered them. He sent them out. "Go and make disciples of all the nations, baptizing them in the name of the Father and the Son and the Holy Spirit. Teach these new disciples to obey all the commands I have given you" (Matthew 28:19-20 NLT). This outward focus, set by Jesus for the first disciples continues to be the perspective of vibrant communities of disciples to this day.

The corporate use of the opening line of Rick Warren's Purpose Driven Life, "It is not about *us*," ought to be the mantra of every community of faith that desires to affect its community for Christ. These communities of faith know that the church perpetually exists for those we would label, "them"—those who reside outside of a relationship with Jesus and a vibrant community of faith. For, as Jesus reminds us, he did not come to call the well, but the sick.

While this perspective is biblically mandated (see MT 4:19; 5:16; 10:1-20; 28:19-20 not to mention the other gospels) and communicates God's heart for the world, it also has inherent benefits *within* the local church.

Internal Benefits

If you are focused outwardly, you can't fight inwardly. We may not be able to agree on the paint colors for the nursery or the carpet for the prayer room. But we can all agree that this message we hold in jars of clay should not be held. It alone has the power to change the world and must escape in order to have its intended effect.

When we are sufficiently focused on those outside the community of faith there is little time for us to disagree about matters inside the community of faith. Show me a church that argues over trivial internal matters and I will show you a church that has little or no focus on what really matters in the Kingdom of Christ—outsiders.

Often one of the most contentious events in the life of a congregation is a building project. There are so many design and preference decisions to make that people end up in sharp disagreements. Churches have split or have been left with a dividing wall of hostility because of strong personal preferences about meaningless matters such as paint colors, bathroom fixtures, and signage.

Throughout the two-year building process and the inhabiting of our first building at The Orchard we had no internal disagreements about what to build, how it should be built, colors, or coverings. That is because we understand that it doesn't matter what kind of structure we are in—we are not building it for us—we are building it for *them*. With this in mind, we did not build to please the people who already attend The Orchard, we built to attract and serve the people who have yet to come—but will!

Most of our congregation did not know what colors, fixtures, or floor coverings were used until the day we moved in—and most did not care. Because, the building is not for us.

This outward focus also helps you prioritize Budget, Energy, Effort, and Buildings. If your community of faith is outward focused it will direct the way that you use the resources available to you.

From The Orchard's inception, we have been focused on helping people grow deep in the love of Jesus, but the equal balance has been on branching out to others with that love. We spend almost four times the amount of money on outreach as we do on discipleship at The Orchard. Of course the main reason for this is that branching out is much more expensive work than growing deep. However, when your focus is on those outside the church your budget can never be satisfied simply to have a line item for evangelism. It is very common for congregations to spend an inordinate percentage of their budgets on themselves. When this is so, there is fertile ground for infighting over available resources. However, when everyone is focused outwardly, there is no competition because a shared perspective moves us all toward a shared desired outcome—reaching the world.

When this is so, not only will your church know how to prioritize its financial resources by balancing growing deep and branching out, it will also know how to spend its collective energy, time and effort.

The first couple of years of The Orchard's existence we met in temporary locations. We did not have to set up and tear down our equipment weekly, however, we did it regularly. In addition, the building we were using needed a significant amount of cleaning weekly. Near the end of our third year, we leased a warehouse and moved in for a four-year stay. During those four years, the intensity of our outward focus skyrocketed. In reflecting on the reason for the increased concentration on missions, we attributed it to the freedom to not have to think about ourselves so much. When we settled in the warehouse we didn't have to think about mass cleanings, moving in or out, setting up chairs or nurseries; we could focus much more of our energies on reaching out. Outward focused congregations make the easy choice of pouring themselves out for others at the expense of navel gazing at themselves.

Moreover, this Outward Focus becomes a measuring stick. One of the most significant moments in my life as the pastor of The Orchard came over the course of a month-long reflection about how we would measure success at The Orchard. I was dealing with the question of evaluation. How do you know if you are doing what you say is important to your organization? What are the measuring sticks?

When we began to try to discern this at The Orchard we first acknowledge what all the potential measuring sticks were. We could have measured our success by looking at the other churches in our community. Were we the largest church in our community? If not, where did we rank? Were we the largest United Methodist Church? If not where did we stand in comparison to other churches in our community, denomination or state? Did we feel we were large enough? And, what exactly was *large enough?* We discovered there were numerous potential measuring sticks and we could create one for almost any criteria that would make us look successful.

The breakthrough came when I was reading Erwin McManus' book an *Unstoppable Force*. He writes: We are accustomed to speaking of the great commission, but it is the commandment that Jesus calls great. The great commission erupts out of the great commandment. The gospel flows best through the establishing of significant relationships that are authentic and healthy. When relationships become stagnant and the community of Christ closes itself to the outside world, the result is an institution rather than a movement.

In a balanced ecosystem, the church has a proper relation-ship to God, and its people have a proper relationship to one another and to an unbelieving world. The measure of our spiritual health must be examined against our steward-ship in relationship to a world that's lost and broken. (*Erwin McManus, Unstoppable Force, 15*)

Our understanding has come to be that: We can never judge the success of our church by looking at the people we do have. We can only judge our success by how we are reaching the people we don't have, *and* by how the people we do have, love the people we don't have.

This astounding truth has radically changed the way that we look at the world and the way we work on our hearts. In chapter 12, I told you the story about a man and his daughter who were told to visit The Orchard because "they will take anybody." This attitude of "we will take anybody" becomes prevalent in congregations where the people understand that we have all been outsiders, and would continue to be so, if Jesus by his suffering, death and resurrection hadn't invited us inside! Therefore, as former outsiders, we now are focused on Christ who is focused on — outsiders.

In fact, that is our measure of success: How many outsiders are left? Our mission will only be accomplished when we are able to answer, "none!"

Don't Dabble, Invest

With that in mind, The Orchard has tried to stay away from Mission experiences that only leave us feeling changed. Those who have been on a mission trip or experience know the euphoria that is part of the experience of being on the trip, but also follows us home for weeks, months and sometimes years. I do not intend to malign these experiences and have had several of them myself. However, it is not uncommon for us to think more about the experience we will have (and craft our mission trips accordingly) than about the change we can affect for Christ's Kingdom.

During the first five years of our existence, we participated in numerous local mission outreaches and traveled to nine different countries, some of them several times, in mission. During year five, it became very apparent to us that we were the ones who were benefiting the most from the mission experiences. Sure, there was some temporary relief in the places we went and the people we served. But we came to discover that the greatest impact was being made in those places where we repeatedly entered into relationships with those we were reaching out too.

With that in mind, we changed our mission strategy to "Don't dabble; Invest." Instead of just going to a foreign mission station once, we changed our strategy in order to repeatedly be in the same places regularly. Instead of being involved in eight or ten local projects, we focused on three and turned up the intensity of our involvement.

Locally we work mostly with a cooperative food bank, with Habitat for Humanity and annual feed the hungry projects.

Instead of nine new countries in the next six years, we are intentionally seeking to develop long-term relationships with mission outposts on every continent in order to have a worldwide perspective. We have already developed these long-term relationships in South America, Western Europe and China. We believe long-term relationships will yield more fruit for Christ's Kingdom than being in many places but only with surface involvement.

Interestingly enough, these long-term relationships also have the strongest effect to keep our focus directed outward. You can neglect the idea of China, but you cannot ignore Paul Cho; You can forget about the idea of Ecuador, but you cannot ignore Lolly Mendoza and her day school full of impoverished children; Your interest can wane in new churches in Zambia, but not if you know that Amos and Setali are counting on you.

This same dynamic is true when you work for months on a Habitat House and are in relationship with the family you are building for or when you work at the food bank and see the same families return for assistance time and time again.

When you are in relationship over the long term, your attention is focused outwardly and your relationship grows inwardly. When the community is knit together by a unified focus outward, disagreements about non-essentials fade away and the essentials—like reaching the world for Christ—become crystal clear.

Conclusion

When Jesus appeared to the disciples in that Upper Room his words to them were "Go." The healthy church looks outward to fulfill that call and in doing so accomplishes both branching out *and* growing deep.

CHAPTER 16

Membership has its Responsibilities

"*M*embership has its privileges!" so said the American Express Commercial of the mid-1980's. That statement is not so profound. We pay for membership in any number of clubs and groups precisely for the privileges that are afforded us when we do. Country clubs, book clubs, music clubs, health clubs, soccer clubs, scrapbooking clubs—there seems to be an endless list of opportunities to purchase privilege and American's take advantage of the opportunities liberally.

Given that there are membership rules that must be followed in order to remain in good standing with our club and thus enjoy the privileges, it is difficult to shift gears when we speak of church membership.

To become a member of a United Methodist Church (my denomination) you need only walk the aisle and pledge your prayers, your presence, your gifts and your service. You don't actually have to fulfill those pledges; you simply have to pledge them at some point. In my opinion, this inconsistency has to do with our inability to think of membership as responsibility rather than membership being about privilege.

I think most persons stand before the church and say with their mouths, "I will support this local congregation with my prayers, my presence, my gifts and my service." But, in their minds their decision to enter into the membership of the congregation was not based on their desire to assume responsibility, but on their estimation of the benefits.

Membership in congregations often affords those families the right to marry in the sanctuary, or to marry in the sanctuary at a reduced cost. It often affords them first opportunity to enroll their children in the church day school or childcare. It gives them access to the facilities and often, greater access to the pastors. In some cases, it even gives them the right to be buried in the cemetery if the church has one. All for simple verbal agreement to a set of questions.

When I first began ministry I think my frustration with this model of membership peaked each year at the time we had to report on membership gains or losses. In every congregation I served before The Orchard our membership was at least three times what our worship attendance was. Each year, it seemed we would discover someone who had been on our rolls for a number of years who was either dead or now a member of another congregation in another city and state. Though frustrated, I had come to resign myself to the fact that church membership rolls were simply that way and there was nothing to be done about it.

That all changed one fall when I visited Ginghamsburg United Methodist Church in Tipp City, Ohio. Ginghamsburg Church required each person who desired to become a member to complete a 12-week class that introduced each participant to the basics of Christianity and the essentials of Ginghamsburg. That idea sparked a hope in me that membership could indeed be different. That it could be about responsibility rather than privilege.

Membership is about Responsibility

Six times a year The Orchard hosts membership classes. It is a three night exploratory class about what it means to be a member at The Orchard. The first night is about history, mission and vision. The second night is about discovering and using your gifts to branch out, and the final night is about finding your place in community and intentionally beginning to grow deep.

I teach the first night and I always begin my time with these words: "Membership is not about privilege. It is about responsibility." I go on to explain that no one is asked to become a member of The Orchard. Membership inquiry is strictly at the interest of the person. We don't care if you ever become a member at The Orchard. In fact, there is only one thing that is available to members that is not available to regular attenders and that is the opportunity to serve in a formal leadership role (i.e. Leadership Team, Jeremiah, Finance Team, Property Team or Personnel Team). Interestingly enough if you asked people who serve on those teams they would not describe their work there as a privilege but as a responsibility!

You can serve anywhere; you can participate in anything and never become a member. But membership's responsibility works two ways. Membership says, "I take responsibility for this community of faith, and this community of faith takes responsibility for me."

For that reason, after completing the three week class those who still desire to become members sign a covenant in which they take responsibility for:

1. A personal relationship with Jesus and being baptized
2. Praying daily for The Orchard its ministries and Staff
3. Committing to our strategy of Worship Plus 2 in which they
   a. Discover and use their spiritual gifts to branch out to others.

   b. Commit to join a Small Group so they can grow
      deep and help others do the same
   c. Attend worship when they are not out of town or
      sick
4. Tithing
5. Assent to the Vision, Mission and Core Values of The
   Orchard, and
6. Invite others to The Orchard, especially those who do
   not attend church anywhere.

And the church takes responsibility for holding them
accountable for this covenant that benefits the community of
faith as a whole and the individuals who make it up.

Measuring the membership
   One of the chief problems with walk-the-aisle commitments is that after that one moment in time, those persons
are never asked those questions again. They are never asked
to assess their progress or the progress of the congregation
in its ministry efforts. Assuming most people are like I am, I
need at least a yearly checkup on my commitments.
   With evaluation and responsibility in mind each February
The Orchard mails to its members a covenant evaluation
card. The card itemizes the very same commitments that
are on the initial covenant they sign. However, under each
of those commitments are two sets of numbers (1-5). One
with which each member evaluates how well they kept the
covenant during the previous year and one with which they
evaluate the staff and church's efforts at helping them do
so. They mail these cards in by March 1 or drop them in the
offering bag, and the staff begins to sort through the cards
getting feedback and identifying members with whom we
need to follow up.

Advantages of high commitment membership

It may seem awkward to many congregations to receive such feedback but it is precisely this annual accountability that keeps the covenant vibrant. It reminds both the individual and the corporate community that we are mutually responsible for the health of the whole. It is perfectly understood that the spiritual health of the whole is vitally tied up with the spiritual health of the individual. Beyond the covenant nature of membership, practical advantages to this way of relating abound.

For starters, the covenant relationship does not let you take the spiritual growth of the members for granted. As much as we would like, we cannot assume that just because people hear our "outstanding" sermons every week that they are growing deeper in the love of Jesus. Nor, can we assume that simply because we are providing opportunities for branching out to others with that love that people are doing so.

When someone evaluates themselves as a 1 (not at all) or 2 (rarely) regarding small group participation, it speaks volumes about their spiritual growth. Similar self-evaluations regarding tithing, serving or praying do the same. When that kind of an evaluation is returned, we know that as a staff we are either missing the mark in ministry (which would show up in a corresponding low evaluation on the second set of numbers) or a person is struggling.

Sometimes we get a high personal evaluation, but a low ministry/staff evaluation. That feedback is just as valuable. Just as we are tempted to take the spiritual growth of our people for granted, we are equally tempted to believe that our ministries are powerful and effective. We all know that this is not the case, but without an evaluation how do you get feedback from the people that those ministries affect the most? Each year we are able to look at the covenant evaluation cards and the ministries we have in place that are working to help people grow in that area and determine if we are being truly effective or simply deluding ourselves.

There are a couple of more distinct advantages to high commitment membership. By developing a covenant and membership class, you let people demonstrate their commitment to the vision, mission and core values of your church.

How would you like to have a list of leaders who, after understanding where you are going, sign on to take the trip with you? Every pastor I know would pay good money for that list. Well, all the list costs you is the discipline to define your mission, vision, and core values; to outline a membership covenant and to set up a membership class. Add to that the covenant commitment evaluations annually and you also know who is growing spiritually and you now have a list of those committed to the call and to personal training so that they may answer it.

Invite people to a new level of commitment

This idea may sound incredibly foreign to a denominational church that has its membership standards set for it by a governing body. Objectors will say, "You can't set up standards that are higher than our rule of law outlines." Actually, you can. Simply create a completely new level of commitment. Still take anyone who wants to come down front and commit their prayers, presence, gifts and service to the church. Then, (or beforehand) tell them about mutual responsibility and ask them to go beyond regular membership to covenant membership. You will be surprised at how many people will take advantage of such a commitment because what people want most may be privilege, but what people need most is to be part of something that is making a difference in the world and in their own lives.

You may want to keep a couple of things in mind when working out a covenant for high accountability membership.

- Don't make your covenant too long. Five or six commitments at the most.
- Be sure the covenant commitments are measurable. You can't measure attitudes, and perceptions.
- Be sure that you include a way to ask people how they are doing at keeping the covenant and that lets them offer feedback to you about your helpfulness in doing so.

Conclusion

Membership has only one privilege and that privilege is responsibility. When we communicate to people that we value them enough to watch out for them spiritually, they will take responsibility for themselves, for the community as a whole, and for the world. This is an intimidating responsibility at times, but it is the privilege of those who follow Jesus.

One Final Thought

*W*hat does it take to make an impact for the Kingdom of Christ? What is involved in being abundantly fruitful (John 15:16) in order to bring great glory to God? I believe there is a one word answer—availability.

It is amazing how the God of the universe chooses to limit himself by the dreams and availability of his followers. But when a no limits God finds no limits followers the miraculous can happen. When we are completely available, when our dreams, our ideas, our understandings, our most cherished beliefs and our most beloved traditions, when our career and our convictions about how "church" can be done, should be done or must be done are available to God, then an unpredictable God breaks in!

If you are available, and the community of faith you serve is available for the Holy Spirit to infuse you with God's dreams, God's ideas, God's understanding, and God's power to fulfill those things—then God will plant and grow an Orchard with you.

Printed in the United States
47447LVS00003B/1-201

9 781600 340017